Susan Beecher   **Woodfired Pottery**

MOUNTAIN ARTS

Catskill Press

Cruet Set, white stoneware with Violite glaze and slips, 8 x 4 x 6 inches, 1998. Woodfired. Appeared in *Ceramics Monthly* International Exhibition, 1999.

For my dearest Mosa,
whose love, guidance and humor
will always be with me

For Mom and Dad,
whose family camping trips taught me to work hard
and to appreciate nature's glory

For Sean and Corrina,
whose caring encouragement
touches me deeply

For my firing team, who are also my family
and who really make it happen

For Mikhail Zakin and Karen Karnes,
who laid the paths

For my teachers
Michael Simon, Jeff Oestriech, Warren MacKenzie,
Malcolm Davis and Michael Boyer,
who gave me so much

For Grace Sullivan, Bruce Dehnert
and Barbara Ravage,
whose contributions to this book
are deeply appreciated.

Studio photography by James Dee
Location photography by Grace Sullivan and Susan Beecher
Color correction by Dave Harrington, Ruder Finn Printing Services
Designed by Grace Sullivan, Catskill Press

Printed by Ruder Finn Printing Services

First published in 2005 in the United States by Catskill Press,
an imprint of Ruder Finn Press, Inc.
301 East Fifty-Seventh Street
New York, NY 10022

ISBN #: 1-932646-10-8

Printed in the United States of America

Contents

Foreword

Dragonfly Teapot
White stoneware with Susan's Green glaze and slips,
7 x 4 x 5 inches, 2004. Woodfired.
In the collection of Mr. and Mrs. Art Klein.

To fully appreciate Susan Beecher's seemingly unquenchable desire to turn a lump of mud into a high-density, flame-kissed lidded casserole stuffed to its gallery with roast lamb in a scrumptious broth, emblazoned with plums and peppers and onions and steaming ready to eat in the middle of your simple oak table on a bitterly cold winter's day, it helps to understand that one of the first times I fired the wood kiln at Peters Valley Craft Education Center I did so to a delicious concert of stories told by Susan's husband, Mosa Havivi. One story that stuck had Mosa, then the 10-year-old son of Russian emigrés, dragging his cello through the sands of Israel to study at the feet of Thelma Yellin. I remember the sweeps of his glorious hands enunciating moments in time gone by, while Susan's hands were busily stoking our belching kiln with northern Jersey hardwoods. What became evident over the course of our firing—and over the six years since then—was that theirs was a true partnership. To this Susan brought her down-to-earth logic explained in a rhapsody of images taken from the natural world around her, while Mosa served up the spiritual quest, the grand gesture of what is possible, though hidden.

It was in the Catskill Mountains of New York that this joining of rhapsody and gesture gave life to Susan's pots. What I've since learned about the Catskill Region is that it is a place where anything is possible. I once heard a Catskill Region farmer quoted as having observed, "reality has never been of much use here." Susan has a pretty good idea of what is meant by that. Driven to make her pots in this place of pine and deciduous forests that go dark in the always approaching winds, she is a dynamo who has surrounded herself with like-minded adventurers, most of them women, all of them friends. And like her many famously tenacious relatives who left indelible marks on American culture, Susan cannot be waylaid or sidelined. Her pots speak volumes about her place and time.

Crediting experiences at Peters Valley for giving her career as a studio potter its jump start, Susan has studied, instructed, and fired here over the course of many years. Peters Valley is a quiet place nestled in the gentle hills of northwestern New Jersey, a stone's throw away from the Delaware River. This art center has played a pivotal role in helping to form many of America's premier potters over the past 35 years. Though spring comes late in the shadow of the Kittatinny Ridge, it is a good time of year to fire the kiln. While the nights are still cold, the light stays longer and the days are ideally cool. Itwas these springtime firings of the double-chambered kiln at Peters Valley that would teach Susan to be patient and what to look for in a flame. And when she was ready, Susan packed up her notebook, thick with pages of observations, and built her own kiln a couple of hours north.

Wood firing is an indigenous practice in most areas of the world where there has been even a semblance of ceramic culture. Here in New Jersey, the Lenape people would have fired their earthenwares in small piles of kindling. The juices and oils of their stewed meats soaked through the porous walls of the pots, sealing them against liquids. The Neolithic tribes of Henan Province in China were firing in this same manner as far back as 6,500 BC. Under the fluorescent green canopy of Borneo's jungle, the Iban have used wood firing to harden their cooking pots for 6,000 years. But the technology that Susan utilizes to achieve oranges like the bellies of salmon and blues like the cove waters of Green County didn't arrive in this country until the Europeans dropped anchor south of Boston. It isn't far from there to the Catskill Mountains, where Susan's kiln is brought up to 2,400 degrees Fahrenheit with thirty hours of steady and deliberate stoking.

Susan's nostalgia is for those real things that tug at our sleeves, those parcels of daily life that keep us grounded. Her gift is as much about the future as it could ever be something about the past. While her pots are part of a folk tradition in appearance, they have come out of an effort that balances life lived on the hectic streets of New York City with the quiet country roads of the Catskill Mountains. Rising from an intense process of calculation and living, they speak quietly about the environment and about just getting on. What is most striking to me about Susan's pots is that they seem relics of a simple life. Through handling them, we are offered honest respite from a hurried existence. These pots are what Susan meant for them to be: simple, direct, and lovingly made in order to be put to good use.

The day Susan Beecher became a potter, I'm sure that she was convinced there would never be any other life available to her. This is because making pots is more than just making pots. It is a dialogue with material that, encompassing all the notions of craft and all the conceits of art, stretches out to embrace what it means to leave a mark on one's world. To potters like Susan, every time a pot has been made, something of substance has changed in the universe, though in an almost unnoticeable way. But potters know it's there, especially when it smells like four sticks of pine in a firebox.

Bruce Dehnert

Peters Valley, 2005

Falling Water Jar, Haynes blue glaze, 4 x 6 x 10 inches, 1998. Fired in the Peters Valley Anagama kiln.

My Journey to Woodfire

Fish Cruet Set
White stoneware with Caribbean blue glaze and slips,
8 x 4 x 7 inches, 2002. Woodfired. Appeared in the tenth Annual
Pottery National Exhibition in 2002.

For me, the magic of woodfiring is that each pot tells the story of what happened inside the kiln. It's something that does not happen in any other kind of firing. Every surface shows the impact of the fuel source—the wood—as well as the flame and the ash it produces. A woodfired pot has a directional quality, reflecting the path of the flame as it travels from the front firebox and swirls around the pot on its way to the back of the kiln. The orange-brown-ness or the tan-ness of the surface varies because some parts of the kiln have a different atmosphere than others. The appearance of the glaze—its color as well as its luster—may differ from one side of the pot to the other. The quality of the surface is affected by the ash, both by where it settled and whether as a sprinkling or as a heavy coat. It's as if the flame has kissed the piece, leaving behind its trace. The result is unique and unpredictable. And endlessly fascinating to me.

With woodfire, I feel that I become one with the process. I make the pot and glaze the pot and then I fire the pot, but the fire is an active force in the creation. I may stack the kiln in a way that I hope will guide the flame path and I may stoke the fire and control the dampers in an attempt to influence the effects of the fire, but the fire is an entity in itself, a far more powerful one than I! Even if I make the same piece over and over, each will usually look different because the wood and the fire have produced a different tonal reaction on the glaze and on the clay itself. It's really miraculous, and I never know how that miracle will look. As I stack the pieces, I may think I know which is going to be my favorite, but it's always a surprise, a gift the kiln gives me.

From Midwestern Childhood to Mississippi Summer

My journey to woodfire really began years before I ever touched a lump of clay. Its origins are in the Midwest, where I spent my early childhood in the home of my paternal grandparents, Margaret Beecher and Alfred Abeles. My mother and I moved to the big white house at 726 Ninth Street in Willamette, Illinois, after my father, Alfred Beecher Abeles, was killed at the end World War II. I never knew my father, who was declared missing in action about one month before I was born, but my grandparents kept his spirit very much alive.

As a living memorial for my father, my grandmother started an organization that helped refugees from the war by organizing

My mother, Shirley Ann Radder, aged 20, with me at the age of 6 months in 1945.

families in our church to sponsor them, take them into their homes, care for them, teach them English, get them into school and get them established in America. It grew to include other churches and synagogues, and also received support from the World Council of Churches. Throughout my early childhood, I lived in a house that was always filled with people of many languages and much goodness. Dinners with lots of people around the table are well remembered.

My paternal grandparents, Margaret Beecher Abeles and Alfred Abeles.

Those were rich and happy years for me. Eventually my grandmother was honored by President Eisenhower and by many organizations for her humanitarian work.

My grandmother, Margaret Beecher Abeles, descended from Lyman Beecher, who, along with his children Henry Ward Beecher and Harriet Beecher Stowe, fought against injustice and for human rights by championing such causes as women's suffrage, abolitionism, evolutionism, and a scientific interpretation of the bible, movements that shaped America in the nineteenth century and continue to influence society today. I was raised knowing I was part of that family and shared its humanitarian heritage. I have tried to live my life in the same spirit.

It was from my grandparents and those early years that I acquired three of the most important touchstones that have guided my life. A a serious love of music first came to me from my grandfather, who played the piano and exposed me to church music and show tunes at a very young age. Later it was reinforced by my stepfather, Bruce, who plays many instruments and filled our house with wonderful music when I was growing up, and still does so today! From my grandmother, I got a strong aesthetic based on her appreciation for folk art, color, and the natural world. And above all, I inherited a strong belief in the power of community as a source of personal strength and as a force for change.

When I was five, my mother remarried, and our small family soon grew to five. Because of my stepfather's work, we moved a lot. I went to a different school almost every single year. I never knew anybody. That was hard, but I think it also gave me an inner strength that has served me to this day.

I was in third grade when we moved to Grandville, Michigan. Our backyard abutted an abandoned stone quarry that had been flooded. My little brother and I would go out in the canoe and paddle around, which made my mother nervous because the quarry was very big and very deep, and it wound around so we were often out of her sight. But we loved it! One day I found a natural vein of white clay in the banks. I have absolutely no idea how I knew it was clay, but somehow I did. I dug some out, brought it home, and started making things in the basement. Mostly, I was making a mess, which didn't make my mother happy either. I was in third grade, and the art teacher got me making things with clay. What I remember is that I liked it. But then we moved again and for the rest

My mother and stepfather with my brothers and sisters and my son.

of my school years I had to make a choice between art and music classes. I chose music, so that was the end of clay.

I met my first husband, Robert Cohen, when he and his group, the New World Singers, came to play at my Dad's restaurant. He was a folk singer who knew hundreds of songs in many languages, and through him I fell passionately in love with folk music. It was the early sixties and we were very much a part of the folk and civil rights movements. In 1964, we went to Mississippi as part of what has come to be called Freedom Summer. The overall goal was to go into black communities—many of them very poor and very rural—to register as many people to vote as possible. But part of the objective was to bring young white students from the North—more than a thousand came that summer—to focus media attention on what was going on in the South. Blacks trying to exercise their constitutional right to vote were beaten and murdered, but those stories were never honestly carried on any national television station or in any newspaper—not even the *New York Times.* Even for white students, children of privilege, going to Mississippi meant risking their lives. It was hard in those days to believe we were in the United States of America. Mississippi was like another country, but the national media and even our national political leaders turned a blind eye to what was happening.

I worked in the SNCC (Student Nonviolent Coordinating Committee) office in Jackson, Mississippi, one of the safer places to be. It was the operations center, where we kept informed about what was going on in smaller field offices throughout the state and kept track of where people were. I was in training in Oxford, Ohio, when word came that Michael Schwerner, James Chaney and Andrew Goodman were missing, in one of the most dangerous counties in Mississippi. As each day went by that we didn't hear from them, we were more and more positive they had been murdered.

That summer had a profound influence on my life, not just because of the brutal murders of those three young men, or the opportunity to do what I knew was important work, but also because I met people who were deeply committed to a cause and who would make the revolutions of that decade—not just civil rights, but also the women's movement, the free speech movement and the antiwar movement. It was all there, some of it just beginning, that summer. So it was radicalizing for me; it was both deeply disturbing to see first hand the racist character of our country and extraordinarily inspiring to see, meet and listen to people who had such greatness. I don't mean just people like

Martin Luther King, Bob Moses and Stokely Carmichael. I mean people like Fannie Lou Hamer, the granddaughter of slaves, the daughter of sharecroppers and the co-founder of the Mississippi Freedom Democratic Party. Later that summer she spoke before the credentials committee of the Democratic National Convention, urging them to seat the Freedom delegates instead of the segregationist delegation sent by the state. She was a woman with tremendous moral courage and a clarity of vision beyond anything I had seen before or since.

One other thing that I have carried from that summer into the rest of my life is the music. Every night Freedom Rallies would be held in local churches. The poorer and the tinier the church, the more stirring the music. The freedom songs were essential to the daily lives of the people exposing themselves to danger by trying to register to vote. Singing those songs actually helped people be courageous and do their jobs. I will never forget hearing Bernice Reagon, who later founded Sweet Honey in the Rock, and Fanny Lou Hamer singing together at one of those rallies. The energy in their voices touched every person there, uplifted us all and gave us all the courage we needed. It showed me the power of music, and to this day, music is central to my life. My studio is filled with music—folk and blues, usually. I strive for a lyricism in the surface and in the gesture of my pots and I believe that music infuses my work.

Clay Calls to Me

The year after our time in Mississippi, my husband got a summer job at Idyllwild School of the Arts, in California. By then, my son, Sean, had been born, so the three of us went out to Idyllwild. Susan Peterson, who is an influential ceramic educator and author of many books on ceramics, was the head of the clay program at Idyllwild. I took classes with her, started reading her books, and saw her collection of pots. Years after I discovered clay in the old stone quarry in Grandville, Michigan, clay was calling to me again.

When we returned to New York at the end of the summer, I found Baldwin Pottery, in Greenwich Village. The owner, Judith Baldwin, had a tremendous amount of knowledge,

My daughter Corrina and son Sean in 1968.

which she was more than willing to share. I did some work in the studio and she mentored me in exchange.

That worked for a while, but in 1966 my daughter Corrina was born. I wanted to work with clay as much as possible, but I didn't want to leave my children. The solution, which sounds crazy now, was to make a studio in the small two-bedroom apartment we lived in. I built a kick wheel in my kitchen, had a little electric kiln out on the balcony, and started doing clay at home. When we moved to a bigger apartment, I had a little more space, so I got two more wheels, and I began giving children's classes. It wasn't easy—I had to clean and vacuum every day because of the clay dust. But I didn't have to leave my kids. They were always in my studio, making clay by my side. It enriched us all.

If I had had the financial wherewithal to start my own studio and make a decent income, I would have, but real life intervened. By then my husband and I had divorced, and I had to support my children. I needed a job. Fortunately a friend who worked in publishing got me an interview at Ballantine Books and I was hired. I started at the very bottom, as a customer service representative, but eventually worked my way up, getting promotions and working in many different departments, learning about the business. I took classes in NYU's publishing program. At the time, all I knew was that I had to support my kids, and one day put them through college, but what I learned in those years has truly helped me run my business as a potter as well.

In those days, publishing was a wonderful business. It was filled with people who were excited about books and learning. I enjoyed it immensely. And that's what I did for the next eighteen years, rising to the executive level and eventually working at Random House, Doubleday and Scholastic. Although I tried to keep my hand in clay, I didn't have the space in my being to make the kind of work I wanted to make. I would try to make pots at night after my children went to bed, but I soon realized I was too tired. I didn't like the pots I was making, and there was no growth, which is a terrible thing. So I gave up making pots.

Taking the Plunge

During all that time, I never stopped thinking about clay. When my children were finally out of college, I realized what I really wanted to do was make pots. So I gave up a very substantial salary and took the plunge. By then I had remarried.

For the first time in my life, I had a true partner, my husband, Mosa Havivi, a gifted musician, world class cellist and fine violin restorer. That meant I had someone to share expenses with, but more important, someone who gave me moral support and a great deal of love. It occurred to me that I might be crazy to try to make a living making pots, but I thought I'd try it for six months and if it was not the right thing, I could always stop and get some kind of job. As it turns out, I never once looked back and said, "Oh, I shouldn't have done this."

That was a very important lesson for me, and perhaps it will be for others. It's true that we are bound by our financial situations, but it is truly possible to make a change to follow our heart's desires. I knew that I would be giving up a comfortable salary for the uncertain income of an independent potter, so before I left my publishing job, I did everything I could to lower my living expenses, pay off my debts, and save enough money to make a studio when the time came. I did continue doing some freelance work in publishing and I worked part time in Mosa's violin shop, but my focus was on learning how to become a good potter.

Tall Fluted Vase, dark stoneware with Luster Shino glaze, 11 x 4 x 5 inches, 1991, fired in my gas kiln. Appeared in the New York State Museum Exhibition of Contemporary Crafts.

I embarked on a program of self-education that continues to this day. The first thing I did was enroll in classes at Greenwich House, which has long had a grand reputation as a pottery school and studio. I signed up for an advanced class, which was a bit nervy of me, but I knew I was no longer a beginner and I wanted to challenge myself. It was my first experience with gas-reduction kilns, so I began hanging out in the kiln room and observing the firings. I took a glaze chemistry class and asked lots of questions. In addition to taking classes and throwing pots, I read and looked at as much as I could. Greenwich House has always had a good library, so I spent a lot of time there reading past ceramics journals. I made notes of what work most spoke to me, and then came up with a list of people whose work I wanted to study and with whom I wanted to study, if I could. And I looked at as much work as I possibly could. It was a great time to be in New York, where it was possible to see extraordinary work, whether it was an exhibition of Hans Coper and Lucie Rie, the great British ceramic artists, or ancient Asian pots at Asia House and the Japan Society, or contemporary potters at what was then

Soy Bottle, porcelain with Amber Celadon glaze, 3 x 4 x 5 inches, 2004. Woodfired.

called the American Craft Museum or at small galleries and exhibitions.

Early on, I focused on ancient pots—beginning with Chinese earthenware from the eleventh century BCE, Mesopotamian and Jomon vessels from 5000–4000 BCE and Egyptian and Iranian vessels from 2000 BCE. I was fascinated by ancient pouring vessels, and their influence can be seen in the small oil-and-vinegar sets and soy bottles that I have been making for the past ten years and will continue to make, I am sure, for at least another ten. I studied the Chinese, Korean and Japanese work of the Ming and Edo periods, Minoware and Oriebeware, which date from the seventh to nineteenth centuries AD, and the eighteenth-century decorated work of Kenzan from the Narutaki kiln. These pots continue to influence my work in subtle ways. I believe that we all—students as well as professional potters—should spend time looking at old pots from other cultures, and revisit them again and again. They have many lessons to teach.

Another important influence on my work was Bernard Leach, a teacher, writer, and philosopher who in the last century almost single-handedly reestablished pottery as a traditional craft in the Western world. He published *A Potter's Book* in 1947, considered the bible of pottery. Along with his partner and colleague Shoji Hamada, Leach shaped the future of the studio potter in America and the world.

Thanks to Susan Peterson, who reintroduced me to clay at Idyllwild, Leach and Hamada came to the United States, visiting many art schools and influencing an entire generation of American makers, among them Peter Voulkos and Warren Mackenzie.

The director of Greenwich House at that time was a wonderful porcelain artist named Kim Dickey, who is now a professor of ceramics at the University of Colorado at Boulder. She brought many major contemporary American potters to Greenwich House to give workshops. I was lucky enough to be able to take workshops with these wonderful makers.

I had decided that there were three people in particular who I wanted to study with, all of whom worked in the Leach-Hamada tradition: Minnesota potters Jeff Oestriech and Warren Mackenzie, who had both served apprenticeships at the Leach Pottery in Cornwall, England, and Michael Simon, who had been a student of Mackenzie's and now lives and works in Georgia. All of them are master potters, and Warren Mackenzie is a living legend. Over the next few years, I managed to take a number of workshops with each one of them, which greatly enriched my vocabulary of making and looking at pots. I also took a workshop at the 92nd Street Y with Malcolm Davis, a contemporary maker who works in porcelain and has a wonderful way of teaching teapots. Each of them in his own way has had a considerable influence on my work and my life as a potter.

A Studio in the Catskill Mountains

In 1986, my husband and I bought a small house in the Catskill Mountains as our retreat from the hectic life of New York City. We both fell in love with the Catskill region. The mountains reminded me of the lakes and forests and hills of the Midwest of my childhood, and the birch forests reminded Mosa of his early years in Russia.

The house had a small horse barn behind it, and it wasn't lost on me that it would make a great pottery studio. So when it became clear that making pots was what I wanted to do, and what I wanted to keep on doing, it also became clear that I needed my own space in which to work. Even though I was still taking classes and workshops, I had to have my studio where I

The barn, before it became my studio.

could make as much as I wanted as big as I wanted whenever I wanted. I was lucky to find a lovely local carpenter, who worked with me to turn a hundred-year-old barn into a studio. It had to be insulated because the winters in the Catskill high peaks are very fierce, and it can

My studio is a restored horse barn that is 100 years old.

be cold even in October and November. I decided it had to have two rooms because I wanted the kiln in a separate room so I wouldn't be breathing fumes as I worked. We began with the first room, where I would do my making, and gradually I had my own studio. I was thrilled. To this day, I love my studio. I can look out the windows and hear my brook and see the forest behind our house. My real home is where my studio is.

Of course, in addition to my own studio, I needed my own kiln. I decided on a gas kiln. I loved gas firing; I was intrigued by the richness and the depth, the marrying of the glaze and the clay surface. I researched gas kilns and talked to a lot of people, and then, with much trepidation, I bought a small Bailey kiln—it holds about sixty-five or seventy-five pots—that I thought would be the kiln I'd use for the rest of my life. Then I started the process of learning to glaze and fire my own kiln. I remember my first firing. It was such a little kiln, but it just seemed monumental to me at that time. Preparing all the glazes was monumental; glazing sixty pots was monumental; the firing itself was terrifying. A lot of the early firings were not great, but I

always had some pots that were decent. I just kept learning, taking notes, talking to people, looking for glazes that were more forgiving, that didn't demand a perfect atmosphere. And in time, I started to consistently get the results I wanted. I guess it's like anything in life: the more you do it, the more you learn and the less monumental it becomes.

I have found that, like most artists, I struggle with how much I need to be alone and how much I need to be with other people. I think my best work comes when I'm working alone, but it's very lonely to work in solitude all the time. So I needed to find a balance.

I have been able to do that, because even after I built my studio in the Catskills, my husband and I spent much of the time in New York City because of his work, and I really needed a place to work when I was there. I found a small studio four blocks from where we lived on the Upper West Side of Manhattan.

That studio has provided such richness to my life because of my dear friend and firing partner Tania Kravath, who runs the studio, and the other women with whom I share it. There are five or six of us. We each have our own small space and we share an electric kiln. Over time, we have done group projects and we have a spring open house. It's a wonderful community. We respect each other's need to work and need to be quiet at times, so it's an ideal mixture of being together, but also being able to work.

Finding My Own Voice

I was still searching for an aesthetic that I would feel totally comfortable with, but I wasn't there yet. It takes a long time to find your own voice in the clay—the thing that makes your work discernible from everybody else's—within the confines of functional pottery. It's a journey; you can't force it to happen fast, but if you keep searching and exploring, you will come to it in time. Although I place myself within the Anglo-Asian tradition of Leach and Hamada, I am still evolving. I hope I will be evolving until the day I die.

Then one year my work was accepted in a number of national juried shows. I had been applying to, and being turned down by, national shows for five years at least. The competition to get into these shows is fierce. The good ones usually get over a thousand entries, and normally take no more than a hundred pots. Finally being accepted was very validating. It also helped get my name more established, and as a result I began to be invited to give workshops and to teach.

Around that time I took a workshop given by Jeff Oestriech at Peters Valley, in Layton, New Jersey. It was so enlightening, not only in terms of what I learned about technique, but also because of what Jeff said about the lifestyle, the tradition and the aesthetics of making. It was also at that workshop that I first encountered woodfiring, but it would be years before I could even dream of having my own woodfire kiln. Some of the pieces that I got out of that firing with Jeff were just marvelous. I loved them and that really made me think a great deal about woodfiring.

Jeff talked about the cycles of a potter's life—the making cycle, the firing cycle and then back again to making. That has stayed with me because those are now the cycles of my life. It's sort of like the phases of the moon or the cycle of the seasons. I feel my life is framed by the cycle I am in.

Oval Jar, dark stoneware with Cushing Copper glaze, 5 x 4 x 11 inches, 1993. Fired in my gas kiln. Juried into the Strictly Functional Pottery National exhibition in 1994.

The Cycles of a Potter's Life

Living through the cycles changes your work. I've found that when I have a long period of making, my pots change and grow in subtle but meaningful ways. By long, I mean two or three months, maybe even four, of doing nothing except making pots. When I'm intensively making work over a period of time, my senses and my touch and my eyes are much more sensitive to the medium. One small thing leads to another. One idea will carry me to another. It isn't always an "aha!" moment, though I do sometimes have those. It is usually much more subtle than that. I might find a different way to make a lip and then want to try that lip on something else. Or one form will suggest another form. Or I will make a series of vases and one vase will stand out. When that happens, I always ask myself: "Why is that one better?" I look at it and I think about it. Perhaps that one's better because of where the waist or the neck falls, or where and how the neck turns in. I might think, "Oh, it would be better with a little handle or a little more belly or a little more volume." If I discover a better proportion, I try it in another piece and see how that works.

This thought process goes on day after day for three months, and for me it becomes part of my dreaming, my earliest morning thoughts, and probably my latest night thoughts, when I'm going to sleep and waking up. Then I am just dying to get into the studio. I never get sick of that pull to the studio. In fact, it causes problems because I don't want to do the mundane things of my life—I don't want to go grocery shopping, I don't want to pay the bills and I don't want to clean the house. I want to be in the studio. It's like a love affair. I become totally immersed, or want to be as much as I possibly can. When that goes on for three months, I am in an altered state.

It's usually then that I have to stop because it is time to fire. Firings are normally dictated by how much work can fit in the kiln, or how much time there is before the next show. So I know I can make only until a certain date, but when I'm in an energetic flow, I never want to stop. Usually after a very intensive period of work, I'm thinking, "Oh, if I could just make one more set of jars," or "It's getting really good; I wish I could make one more series," but alas, I have to stop because I have to start firing.

Pagoda Box, white stoneware with flashing slip, 6 x 6 x 11 inches, 1992. Fired in the Peters Valley wood kiln in a workshop with Jeff Oestriech.

Double Lip Bowl, porcelain with Yoder's Blue glaze, 8 x 8 x 5 inches, 1991. Fired in my gas kiln.

For me, decoration is part of the making cycle because I do surface decoration when my pots are leather hard, just after trimming and putting on handles. I find that the slip moves more easily over leather-hard clay. I'm always striving for a soft fluidity in my pots, and I feel that if I decorate at that stage I'm closer to getting that.

In this period of my making, I decorate about eighty percent of my pots. In the early years at Greenwich House, I didn't decorate at all. I was working with gas-reduction glazes, and I might use glazes in combination or a wax resist technique, but I never decorated—I never thought I could decorate. That came much later when I started doing wood firing. It developed out of one of the things that moves me most about woodfiring: the interplay between the areas that are glazed and the unglazed areas, which have a luscious rust-brown-tan-orange surface that you can't get in any other kind of firing.

Decoration has become integral to my making process. When I am throwing the pieces, I am already thinking about how I'm going to decorate and glaze them. Each series takes off from what I've done before. So, for instance, I know that on a series of pitchers I want the decoration to flow diagonally because I feel that gives the pitcher more movement, and I can make it flow off the handle, down the form.

I was never natural with the brush. In fact, I froze up when I'd get a brush in my hand. But my son, Sean, who was making pots for a while, was absolutely natural with the brush. Any mark he made was loose, fluid and just wonderful. I was so envious. When we were in the studio together, he just kept encouraging me. "Mom, you can do it. Just take this brush and just practice." So I started practicing, first on paper, but with ceramic slip or black EZ Stroke so I would have a feel for the medium. Then I practiced on pots, many of which ended up being recycled or going to the dump. But I started decorating—just lines at first. And I liked it even though it was such a challenge. I always tell students that it took me five years to make a good leaf, and maybe ten years to make a good branch, but I keep trying.

I started making birds around 2001 when I was teaching in Florida during the winter and working in a small studio I had set up on an old screened-in porch. I would see majestic snowy egrets just walking by, as proud and

Ovaled Bottle with Birds, white stoneware with Violite glaze and slips, 4 x 3 x 7 inches, 2005. Woodfired.

elegant as anything you've ever seen. My husband and I were enraptured with them, and I thought, "Well, I have to put some birds on my pots." So I started trying to make birds. And I'm still trying to make birds. Some of them are good and some of them are not.

When I'm decorating, I try to put some sort of emotion into these little creatures on my pots, some expression of human feeling and interaction. I imagine they tell a story. It's usually a story about friends or a couple and they're either in love or flirting or trying to be in love, or they're mad.

Most of my decorative motifs are from nature, and they all have meaning in my life. I make cattails, for instance, because cattails grow everywhere in the Catskill Mountains, where my studio is. I make fish because fish and water have spoken to me all my life. Fish are also a universal symbol of peace and brotherhood, so that's what I'm thinking about when I make fish. Also I'm thinking about the thousands of majestic fish such as the Blue Finn Tuna that are disappearing from our oceans. The blueberries come from my daughter, who grows luscious sweet berries on her organic farm in northern California. The dragonflies come from an almost mystical experience my daughter and I had together. One day when I was visiting her, we hiked through the forest up to a glacier lake. As we emerged from the forest we could see thousands of dragonflies dancing and fluttering on the surface of the lake. I got chills through my body as we watched those dragonflies: they were red and iridescent blue and they were just diving and bobbing up and down over the water. So when I put dragonflies on my pots, it's not because they're a popular motif; it's because they recall that magical encounter.

An underlying theme in all these things—birds, fish, blueberries, dragonflies—is nature. It expresses a very serious concern I have that we humans are quickly making this planet uninhabitable for beautiful creatures. I continue to be deeply concerned about our environment.

Decorating ends the making cycle. The firing cycle begins with a lot of separate tasks that take an entirely different kind of energy, a different kind of attention. I have to get the pots all dried, and hope they're drying without cracks. Then they have to be bisqued. Meanwhile, I have to get the glazes ready, and that's a very

Dragonfly Vase, white stoneware with Susan's Green glaze, 5 x 4 x 9 inches, 2005. Woodfired.

exacting process—one small mistake of a single ingredient can ruin a whole batch of pots. I always try to make glazes in the morning, when I'm fresh, and I do it with the utmost care.

I don't let anybody else make my glazes, because if there's a mistake, I want to be the one who made it.

I feel I could spend many lifetimes on glazing—finding new glazes, making glazes, testing glazes. I've always had a rule, in every period of my making—for an electric kiln, for a gas kiln, and now when I'm making for the wood kiln—to test something new in every firing. It might be a new glaze recipe, a new combination of glazes, a new slip under a glaze. That's how we learn, that's how we figure out what works and what doesn't work, what we like and what we don't like.

Woodfiring is substantially more involved and time-consuming than electric or gas firing. I've devoted an entire section of this book—"Loading, Firing and Unloading"—to showing what the firing cycle is about (see page 57). When the firing begins I have to come back to working closely with others, because woodfiring takes a whole team of participants. One of my goals in building my own kiln was to establish a community of potters and people who enjoy them. It's part of my grandmother's legacy, I am sure. The communal sense of discovery and

accomplishment that ends the firing cycle is, to me, one of the greatest delights. It gives me great joy to share it.

I'm always sad when people start packing up their pots to take them home. I don't want anyone or the pots to leave. But life must go on. I keep my pots out in the yard for a few days, especially in the summertime. Even though I don't advertise my firings, word has gotten out and local people stop by to look and to buy. Finally, I move the pots to the little showroom behind my studio or pack them up to go to galleries or shops or to a show.

And that's the end of the firing cycle. By the time it's over, all I want to do is get back in the studio and try to make something similar to what I loved from the firing. Those results spur me on, so I can't wait to get started making another 200 pots for the next firing.

My Enchantment with Woodfire

In the mid-1990s, a number of years after I was introduced to woodfiring by Jeff Oestriech, Peters Valley with its two-chamber Noborigama kiln was my woodfire home.

In addition to Jeff's workshop there, I attended several with Frank Martin, a real glaze guru who was Head of the Ceramic Studio at the 92nd Street YMCA in New York City, an excellent clay program. Later I would join a group of other potters and rent the Peters Valley kiln, and eventually I put together my own group with my New York studio mates Tania Kravath and Sara Patterson. Peters Valley was a sheltered environment because we had Bruce Dehnert, the extremely knowledgeable Head of Ceramics and a superb teacher, to guide us through the firings. Bruce was totally open and forthcoming with information, and I will always be grateful to him because he taught me a tremendous amount. I also did a firing in a smaller one-chamber kiln with Louise Harder. I would learn something new from each person I woodfired with. I was swept away by the possibilities and the aesthetic of wood fire, but I still wasn't thinking about having my own wood kiln, because I knew it is an incredibly difficult and challenging undertaking, a huge commitment and very hard physical work.

I was trying to stay open to other atmospheric aesthetics that might please me as much as

Box with Fish, white stoneware with Rob's Green glaze, 5 x 5 x 7 inches, 1999. Soda fired in Mikhail Zakin's kiln.

woodfiring. So with that in mind, my friend Malcolm Davis introduced me to Mikhail Zakin, an extraordinary maker and educator who founded the Old Church Cultural Center and School of Art in Demarest, New Jersey. She invited me to teach at Old Church and became a wonderful mentor to me. I'll never forget the nights we sat around her house waiting for the kiln to move while she told marvelous stories about her early years, becoming a sculptor and metalsmith. Mikhail has had an extraordinary career, teaching and traveling all over the world. In the fifties, she and Karen Karnes were among the first to revive traditional salt firing in the United States. It was widely practiced in Europe and America in the seventeenth century. The "orange-peel" surface that characterizes salt firing results when salt is introduced into the kiln at different points during the firing. The high heat causes the sodium chloride to break down into its component elements. The sodium combines with the silica in the clay to produce a glazed surface while chlorine escapes as exhaust. Karen Karnes later went on to woodfiring, but Mikhail stayed with salt and soda pots. I am immensely grateful for all she has shared with me over the years and to this day.

Despite the richness of my time with Mikhail, salt and soda firing did not hold the magic for me that woodfiring did. At some point, I realized that I could no longer make pots unless it was for woodfire. And that's when I realized I wanted to have a kiln of my own. It was a big step financially and I knew I would have to accept sacrifices in other parts of my life. I began investigating possibilities and thinking hard about the challenge I was setting for myself.

There are many different styles of wood kilns, and the choice depends on many factors, including how long you want to fire, how much ash you want on your pieces, if you are going to use a lot of glaze or not much glaze or no glaze at all. The Peters Valley kiln gave me the aesthetic I desired, so that was the kiln I decided I wanted to build.

So I wrote to Will Ruggles, who with his wife, Douglass Rankin, designed and built the Noborigama kiln at Peters Valley, as well as the one at Penland, in North Carolina. He sold me the plans for the kiln, which included a materials list. And he was especially helpful during the building when we had questions. Next I set about finding experienced kiln builders to turn the plans into reality. At a 2000 conference called Utilitarian Clay, I met Julie Crosby, who had built a number of kilns with Nick Gaeta and Steven Morowitz. While I was waiting to hear whether Julie and her partners were willing to sign on, I started a months-long quest for the bricks and other materials I needed—the best I could find for the least amount of money. This was not as easy as I thought it would be.

The next issue was where to place the kiln. I didn't want the kiln to be too far from my studio because carrying all the work would be an arduous chore. I have a brook on the left side of my studio, so the kiln could not go there. I chose the only other possible site, on the right side of my property. It's a bit farther from the studio than I'd like but it's at a legal distance from the property line and also near enough to my garage that I could bring electricity to the kiln site from the garage and also use it as a way station during wet weather. I got a building permit, assembled a team of friends and potters to help with the actual building, and by August we were ready to go. It was an amazing adventure in its own right. The steps involved can be seen in "Building the Dream Kiln," beginning on page 42.

This small stream runs behind my studio. I never tire of the lovely babbling noise that it makes.

We worked for two weeks straight without pause and got everything done except for the chimney, then took a week off to rest and finished a week later. The day the kiln was completed, we had a little ceremony. Mosa brought out a flag and we saluted the kiln and just gazed in admiration. The soft curved lines of the chambers were so lovely. I was in love with her. Yes, it's a she. We named her Lucy, after Julie's dog.

Our first firing was in October 2001. It was difficult and long: it took about thirty-five hours. It may be because it was the first and also that we were firing in the way we'd learned from the Peters Valley kiln, because we thought, well, it's the same kiln. But my kiln behaved differently. In fact, every kiln has its own identity. Materials vary, geographic location varies. That was certainly true in this case: We were up in the mountains and the Peters Valley kiln is in a valley. So we began thinking about possible modifications and made one or two small ones, but we wanted to have one more firing before we began making too many changes.

The second firing, which was over Thanksgiving weekend, was a fateful firing. The weather was calm when we started, but then a huge storm blew up, with winds blowing at least fifty miles an hour. I had a roof over my kiln but no shed. We were quite a few hours into the firing when the storm began. We should have stopped, I now know, but we all had pots in there for our Christmas shows, because that's what potters do in November, that's when you can make money.

So we just kept going. Because of the terrible conditions, we used a lot of wood and there was a lot of smoke, but finally, after about forty hours, we got to temperature more or less. It was exhausting, but when it was over I thought it was over. We had our Christmas pots and all was well.

Then, a couple of weeks into January 2002, I got a phone call telling me that my neighbor had filed a complaint against my wood kiln because of the smoke. I apologized profusely and said that I would by all means notify him when I planned to fire, or even agree upon firing dates when he and his family would not be there. But my neighbor rebuffed these conciliatory gestures and even refused to speak to me, referring me instead to his lawyer. I was summoned to a meeting of the town board. I came with my husband and my neighbor came with lawyers. I was expecting an opportunity to reconcile and of course publicly apologize for the smoke and any other inconvenience I had caused; the lawyers demanded the kiln be shut down. The upshot was that the town decreed that I could not fire until further notice.

There ensued a two-year legal battle, during which time I was unable to fire the kiln. I was in shock. I went back to renting the Peters Valley kiln, which was a huge financial hardship, as I had put over $25,000 into building the kiln and then was unable to even begin to recoup my investment by firing it.

The outlook was really bleak. My town is very small, and with all small towns, politics can be byzantine. There was no telling what would happen. There were moments when I thought, "My god, am I going to lose this case and never be able to fire my kiln again?" But then there were other times when I thought, "Well, maybe I will win this."

Then something truly heartwarming happened. I began to get calls from people in the town and surrounding area who were appalled by what had happened and wanted to come to my defense. Many of them spoke up for me at a series of open town meetings where the entire issue was debated. In addition, I got a lot of support from other potters. Many potters wrote letters to the town, including Jack Troy, who is the father of American woodfiring and who wrote a long letter in defense of me and my kiln. His words, which were both heartfelt and authoritative, meant a great deal.

After visits from the fire and housing departments as well as the state department of environmental protection, all of which found my kiln to be in compliance with every regulation on the books, and hearings that went all the way to the state supreme court, the case was finally decided in my favor in February 2004. Two years and many thousands of dollars later, I had my kiln back.

The town did require that I build a kiln shed. So I did that, and boy, am I glad I did! Every time it rains or blows really hard and we can fire my kiln inside my kiln shed, we say thank you to my neighbor.

The Journey Never Ends

The whole ordeal taught me some important lessons, among them that there are a lot of wonderful people in my local community as well as the wider community of potters. When I built my kiln, one of my dreams was to build a community of people who like to fire with wood. I also wanted to show young people what a traditional pottery studio and kiln looks like and how it all works. I think it's important to save these traditional ways of making in a modern world and to share them with others.

I believe that we all have a wish to recreate the goodness of our early years. I know I do. My efforts to create community around clay arise from my deep belief that clay—indeed involvement in any craft—can change a person's life for the better. I've seen it with my students over and over. I think what I try to do in the classroom and with the community that I'm building around my kiln is linked with what my grandmother was doing back in Illinois so many years ago.

At this point, I have fired my wood kiln only nine times, so I still have much to learn and a long way to go. The journey never ends. Every cycle of making pots brings me to a new place as I explore what I'm making, what changes I want to make or what new things I want to try. My life is enriched by this process of making, and I'm grateful for it.

In all the stages of my journey, Mosa, my beloved partner, was by my side, always encouraging. He never said, "How can you do this? It's too huge, it's too disruptive." He loved the community of artists who came to our home, and he loved seeing the artwork. His favorite thing was to go out after a firing and look at all the pots and talk to people about their work. He had incredibly good eyes and would share what he saw about the work. And he loved the potters' dinners. We would have such a good time around the table, sharing delicious food while he told his stories, such great stories. There just aren't words to say how much that meant to me.

Mosa died on December 13, 2004. It's very lonely without him, but I think he knew this day would come and his supporting me to have the kiln was his way of helping me live through my loss.

Susan Beecher with **Barbara Ravage**

East Jewett, New York, 2005

Mosa Havivi
Cellist, instrument restorer, humorist, storyteller and beloved by family and friends.

Building the Dream Kiln

Building my kiln was a daunting task for me. Not only was I concerned about the expense, which was considerable, but I was also worried about taking on a big construction project when I had never been involved with building anything before. But I wanted this kiln as much as I had ever wanted anything in my life, so there was no choice but to move ahead. Fortunately, my kiln builders were very experienced and this gave me courage. My hope is that the following photos and captions will give you a general idea of what goes into building a high-fire wood kiln. So if you decide to build your own kiln, at least you can start with some notion of what will happen!

After I received my building permit, having spent months studying, planning, and searching out sources for materials, the building was to begin. I had three kiln builders who had solid experience in building this kind of kiln and my instinct was that we would work well together. Friends who were potters were eager to come and labor, and this was certainly appreciated. I found out who was known for precise excavation work in my area and he came with his crew and bulldozers. In a few days the cement foundation was poured, dried and finished. Then the different kinds of bricks and building materials started arriving. Thought had to be given to where to put 7,000 bricks so they would be out of the way but also within convenient reach of the building site. A frightening moment came when the semi truck arrived loaded with bricks and the driver got out, walked up my long driveway, shook his head and said, "I don't think I can get my truck up this driveway. I have no way to turn around!" Thanks to his willingness, we finally worked out a path, but I thought hard about hundreds of bricks left at the side of the road that we might have had to carry to the kiln site. I will always be grateful to that driver, and before he left I thanked him with gifts of pots.

I rented a wet saw with a diamond blade for cutting the bricks. Many of the bricks still had to be cut by hand, however, and this was a skill that the kiln builders had to teach those of us who were less experienced. I was impressed over and over again with the precision and care of my builders, who were wonderful to work with.

Little by little and step by step, the kiln grew. The work was exhausting and I spent a great deal of time cooking for the hungry crew. Everyone had to eat, after all.

Perhaps the most exciting part was the creation of the arch form and the construction of the arches of the kiln. I had read about this in books, but the actuality of building the arch form out of wood, placing it, building up the bricks around it and finally taking out the form and having the arch standing still and beautifully firm

Sunset at the kiln site in the Catskill Mountains.

was just miraculous. It was a fabulous moment that I will never forget.

Finally, after three weeks of incredibly hard work, the kiln was completed. It was beautiful indeed, more beautiful than I had ever imagined. Our satisfaction was immense. Now I thought only of firing.

1 Nick Gaeta and Steve Morowitz, potters and kiln builders, clearing the spot for the kiln. Excavation and pouring of the cement foundation had already been completed.

2 A load of bricks arrive for the building. We used 7,000 bricks in all.

3 The site is made ready for the first layer of bricks.

4 Julie Crosby, potter and kiln builder, cuts bricks by hand.

5 Julie and Nick begin to place the first layer of floor bricks. These cement blocks are used to allow air to circulate under the kiln, keeping the foundation cool.

6 Placement of the first layer of cement blocks is finished. It is vital that the first layer is laid perfectly, as the rest of the kiln flows from this beginning. The tents were used to give the kiln builders some shade from the hot summer sun.

7 The next layers of soft brick are laid.

8 Sara Patterson lays high-heat-duty hard brick on the face of what will be the fire box, the area in the kiln that takes the most direct heat. Large tiles were used for the floor of the chambers.

9 Work goes on at night after dinner. The kiln builders start to put up the bag walls.

10 The interior of the main fire box and the bag walls are completed. The bag walls force the flames to separate and travel through the kiln.

11 The front face of the main fire box is built. The lower openings are called mouse holes. These are used for ventilation and to start the initial small fires used to build up coals under the large grate. In the upper line of five holes, stainless steel pipes will be inserted. The pipes will serve as a fire grate for supporting larger logs.

12 The curve of the main fire box requires that a mold be created and castable cement used.

13 Julie smooths the cement after the mold is removed.

14 The crew makes traditional cone-shaped bricks by hand to be used on the curved top of the main fire box.

15 The handmade bricks dry in the sun before being fired in the gas kiln.

16 Nick checks and rechecks measurements to be sure all are correct before laying the handmade bricks. Note the plywood form inside the kiln that supports the curve. This will be burned away later.

17 Laying the cone-shaped bricks is a tough job. They do not want to stay where they are put!

18 Finally the main fire box is finished. The cone-shaped bricks create its curved top.

19 The base of the chimney is in two separate halves which will join to form a single flue higher up the chimney. This allows for better control of one side of the kiln or the other by means of the two separate dampers.

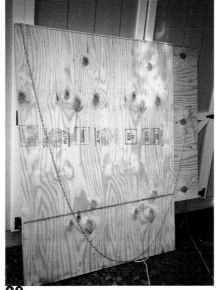

20 The arch forms are created by suspending a chain on a sheet of plywood and tracing the resulting perfect curve onto the wood. The wood is then cut along the outline of the curve. This becomes the curved arch form and ultimately the curve of the kiln chamber.

21 The arch form being completed with help from Sara, Ranley and Steve.

22 The kiln site is readied for the arch form to be put in place.

23 The bricks are built up against the form and held together with a very thin mortar. This allows the kiln to expand and contract during firing with the intense rise and fall of the heat.

24 The arch of the first chamber has dried and the crew is ready to pull out the arch form. We're all holding our breath!

25 Relieved smiles as the arch form is out and the chamber arch is standing.

26 Nick and Julie enjoy a moment of satisfaction upon completion of both chamber arches.

27 The chimney stepping in gradually from two separate sides to a single flue.

28 Nick and Steve work on the back side of the chamber. The soft brick must be cut by hand to match the curve of the chamber.

29 The front of the chambers with the door frame in place.

30 Close-up of door side of chamber, almost finished.

31 Steve and Julie, ready to put the iron rods up on the kiln. These will be screwed together on the front and back of the kiln and attached to a metal rod extending all the way through the kiln, giving added strength to the chamber construction.

32 Julie and Nick working late in the night to build the stone steps.

33 The stone steps, almost completed.

34 Rolls of heat resistant fiber are unwrapped around the kiln. Protective clothing and masks are a necessity when working with this material.

35 After the fiber is on, chicken wire is wrapped over it for added stability and the wire is pinned in place.

36 The entire outside of the kiln is covered with fiber and chicken wire.

37 Large amounts of fire clay, sand and cement are mixed together for the coating of the kiln. Note masks worn by the crew. The dust from these substances is very unhealthy when inhaled.

38 Julie uses her hands and a trowel to put the clay coating on the kiln.

39 The coating is almost complete.

40 The coating on the back side of the kiln.

41 Daisy takes a much-needed nap.

42 The kiln is complete and the crew is very happy and proud.

43 Susan's dream is complete. Now for the challenge of firing!

Casserole with Ferns, white stoneware, Susan's Green Glaze and slips, 11 x 9 x 10 inches, 2004. Woodfired. Exhibited in Strictly Functional Pottery National 2005, a juried show.

Blueberry Platter, white stoneware, slips, blue glaze, 12 x 12 x 12 inches, 2004. Woodfired.

Square Sugar Jar and Creamer, white stoneware with Korean Celadon glaze, 1999. Soda fired.

Cruet Set with Birds, white stoneware, Caribbean blue glaze and slips, 9 x 5 x 7 inches, 2004. Woodfired.

This shed, designed by James Learnihan in 2001, protects the two-chamber Noborigama kiln inside.
The double doors on all sides provide for plenty of air circulation when firing.

Loading, Firing and Unloading: Process and Ritual

The process of firing the two-chamber Noborigama wood kiln is brimming with magic. It is also complicated and enormously challenging, involving a number of detailed activities and a great deal of physical labor. I hope the brief description that follows will indicate just how complicated and thrilling this process can be.

The work begins with the wood. Before doing anything else, we must find, cut and stack all the wood we will need in neat piles for easy access during the firing. Hard and soft wood must be kept separate because of the different effects they have on the fire.

Stacking the pots in the kiln chambers is a painstaking process that normally takes several people most of a day to complete. This kiln holds approximately 350 pots. The placement of each pot, the amount of space between the pots and the arrangement of shorter and taller shelves must all be considered carefully. These variables can seriously affect the length and aesthetic results of the firing, so time is well spent in stacking thoughtfully.

The stacking is very much a ritual, with different people taking on different responsibilities and weaving past each other in and out of the chamber area as they go about getting things done. It almost becomes a dance. The magic enters in when it becomes clear that hundreds of pots by different makers have managed to fit together perfectly on the shelves, and suddenly the chambers are finished.

The actual firing, which demands 20 (or more) hours of methodical stoking, is simply amazing. The fire takes on a life of its own. From its first small crackling sounds to the roaring blaze it becomes in its last hours, it is utterly fascinating. Sometimes we look through the spy hole and actually see the flame and heat flowing through and around the pots like a river. The fact that the pots survive the fire and come out looking beautiful is quite astounding.

Firing continues until the peak temperature of 2,350° F is reached throughout both chambers. Then we completely seal the kiln with bits of fiber or clay so that it will cool slowly.

After four days of cooling, we unbrick the doors and unstack the pots from the kiln chambers, which is mostly a joy. The team is happy and expectant but also a bit anxious. Hidden in our thoughts is the fear that the firing may not have turned out well. But once the doors are unbricked and we can see the pots magically transformed by the fire, what a glorious feeling that is!

Given the detailed orchestration of intense labor it involves, this process requires a team of people held together by fascination with the fire as well as a deep desire to achieve an aesthetic that only wood firing can produce. The group of people I work with have become a close-knit community of artists with tremendous dedication to attending to each other's needs and tremendous acceptance of demanding physical labor.

Very few activities today bring people together to work so intensely for a common goal. Each of us is challenged in different ways by the hours spent concentrating on the fire, the frustration when the firing gets especially difficult, the attempt to understand the needs of our colleagues and the debilitating fatigue that sets in after 20 hours of hard work. All these challenges tend to make one crabby or short-tempered. But the ability of this community of people to rise to the challenges and remain sharp-minded, humorous and deeply understanding of each other is a true testament to our human abilities. In addition to the small core group that participates in every firing, I regularly invite some new and carefully chosen artists to take part, so that more people who are interested have a chance to directly understand this historical experience and the aesthetic it involves. A great part of the magic is the coming together of this community of artists to work together on this challenging activity. Some of the people on my team don't even make pots. They just love to fire!

On the day of unstacking, word of mouth brings people from the surrounding area out to the kiln. They come to look at the new pots and make some purchases, and in this way the magic spreads.

Blueberry Box, white stoneware with Violite glaze and slips, 5 x 5 x 7 inches, 2000. Woodfired. In the collection of Mrs. Beth Kruvant.

Carolyn cleans the kiln thoroughly before we start loading. We need to make certain that there is no debris in the kiln that could land on the pots during the firing.

left: We make cone packs prior to each firing. They must be flawless, because they serve as an important tool for reading the temperature of the fire. The cones are identified by color, and each type melts at a different temperature. By comparing the progress of the cone packs on the door side and back side of the kiln, as well as those on top and bottom, we are able to see whether the kiln is firing evenly.

right: The shelves belonging to the front chamber and the second chamber are kept separate. Because they will be close to the firebox, the front shelves must be washed with alumina solution to protect them from ash. Less ash enters the second chamber, and the shelves are left unwashed.

left: The chamber and shelves are clean and ready for stacking. We brush a solution of alumina hydrate and water onto the bricks to protect the kiln.

right: Portable and permanent shelves hold the glazed pots at the front of the kiln ready for stacking. Pieces are organized by height as much as possible in order to facilitate the stacking of the chambers.

upper left: Ashes must be cleaned out of the firebox before the firing.

right: The glazed pots and stacked wood, ready to go.

lower left: This ash wood was scrap from a baseball bat factory. I always use clean scrap wood for economical and ecological reasons. All the wood must be cut to 40-inch lengths so that it will fit the length of the firebox and produce an even flame. The wood is cut and stacked well before the firing day.

Wadding serves to prevent the bottoms of the pots from sticking to the kiln shelves. The wadding mixture is made of alumina hydrate and EPK clay wedged together to a soft consistency.

left: Wadding begins with rolling coils and cutting them into even, small pieces.

right: The small pieces are shaped into balls of even sizes—smaller ones for small pots and larger balls for larger pots.

left: The balls of wadding are evenly spaced and glued to the bottom of each pot.

This is a time-consuming and tedious job, but it must be done or the pots would get stuck to the kiln shelves due to the ash blowing through the kiln.

right: After wadding all those pots we are ready for a lunch break.

Stacking the kiln starts in earnest with finding the right size of stacking brick for the shelf.

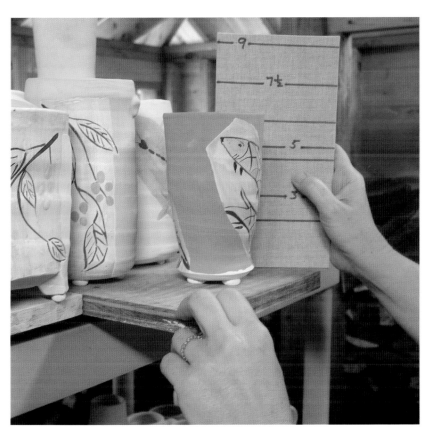

left: Carolyn made a measuring board to help us size the stacking bricks and pots for each shelf.

right: The chamber is completely stacked. Approximately 200 pots fit in each chamber.

left: We coat the door bricks with a thin kiln wash so that they will not become fused during the firing.

right: Sara bricks up the door as tightly as possible and checks to make sure that the cone packs are visible through the peepholes.

We sit down to enjoy a delicious roast turkey
dinner and warm friendship after a long day of
work. No one said wood firing would be easy!

top: A good omen at the start of the firing: a giant blue heron flies over the kiln site.

left: We start by building the fire gradually through the front "mouse holes" of the main firebox, building up an ash bed and heating the air that is sucked into the kiln. The slowness and steadiness are crucial because sudden changes in temperature will make the pots explode.

The steel pipes above the mouse holes serve as a grate for larger pieces of firewood. These will be added through the larger stokeholes on the sides of the main firebox.

right: The doors of the kiln shed are kept wide open during the firing to allow plenty of air to be drawn into the main firebox at the front of the kiln.

top left: Ranley stokes the fire in the main firebox with a mixture of hard and soft wood.

lower left: As the fire is drawn around the chamber and reaches the top, it will shoot out of the blowholes. The appearance of the flames in the blowholes is often used to time the frequency of the stokes.

top right: Sara stokes a "flame thrower": by inserting the wood slowly and gradually rather than all at once, she increases the size and intensity of the flame in order to send the fire up to the top of the chamber.

lower right: At certain times during the firing we withdraw some coals from the main firebox in order to increase air circulation.

This kiln shed, which Jim Learnihan and I designed, has worked wonderfully. Large doors open on all sides for excellent ventilation. When mountain storms and winds come up, they can be closed to protect the kiln from turbulence. The shed also has room in the back to hold the cut wood and keep it dry. Firing with wet wood should definitely be avoided!

The back of the kiln holds the dampers and the chimney. Two separate dampers control each side of the kiln. At the start of the chimney, bricks are in the passive damper. An extra set of dampers lean against the kiln on the floor.

left: Sometimes the firing team has to stay energized with a little dancing. Here Tanya and Ranley have some fun.

right: During the last hours of the firing, we time the stokes by watching the flames as they appear in the damper and the chimney. It is quite hot back here by this time, so I have a cold wet towel around my neck.

After the firing is finished, the kiln is allowed to cool undisturbed for three or four days. Then we unbrick the chamber doors. That first moment of seeing the glorious sight of the finished pots sparkling in the sun is a totally joyous one.

We unstack the pots from the chamber in a slow and methodical manner, with attention to locations within the chamber where especially beautiful results were attained.

left: This green vase shows fine firing results. The glaze has a luminous quality and there are a lot of crystals in it from slow cooling. The clay area is a rich, warm light brown.

upper right: We place the pots on the tables in the order in which they were stacked in the chamber so that we can study the results.

lower right: Three beautiful lidded casseroles by Sara Patterson.

upper left: This amber glazed plate with a wax resist design shows the range of the glaze color: from yellow (where the glaze was thin) to brown (where the glaze was thicker in application).

lower left: I made the bird design that decorates this large bowl by pouring the glaze to give it an abstract feeling.

right: This large lidded casserole shows a beautiful sprinkling of ash on the areas where there is no glaze. This is a very desired effect in wood firing.

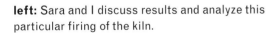

left: Sara and I discuss results and analyze this particular firing of the kiln.

right: I was quite pleased with the results of my glaze application on this platter. The effect was produced by pouring on a white glossy glaze and then pouring a blue wood ash glaze over it.

upper left: The small oval dish in Sara's hand is covered with crystals, which have formed in the glaze during the slow cooling of the kiln. This kind of crystallization happens often during slow cooling, and is another much desired effect of woodfiring.

lower left: A beautiful bowl by Carol Lewis. The medallion design was created with slips and wax resist.

right: In order to have a good firing it is important to have pots of many different sizes, so the kiln can be stacked as evenly as possible. The little pots that can fit in small places are just as important as the big ones.

top left: Sara Lewis reflects on the pots.

lower left: I threw this bowl round with a double lip, then ovaled it and gently pinched the lip to create the design. Note the beautiful crystals in the glaze. See the "Giving Yourself a Lesson" section for information on how to make this oval dish.

upper right: Neighbors come to the unloading to choose pots.

lower right: Friends and family enjoying the riches of the firing.

upper left: Two plates from the firing.

lower left: We never tire of talking about pots. Plans for the next firing are already starting to take shape.

right: A satisfied firing team! Top, from left: Tania Kravath, Carol Grocky Lewis, Ranley Bent, Susan Beecher, Michelle Myers. Below, from left: Carolyn Chadwick, Maureen Donovan, Sara Patterson.

Reflections on Spring, white stoneware with glazes and slips, 20 x 10 x 9 inches, 2001. Woodfired. Appeared in the Utilitarian Clay National Exhibition, 2002. In the collection of the artist.

Bowl with Bird, brown stoneware, Old Yellow and Susan's Green glazes, 12 x 12 x 5 inches, 2004. Woodfired.
In the collection of Mr. and Mrs. Allan Burton.

Stormy Weather Platter, white stoneware with Blue Ash glaze and Buttermilk glaze, 11 x 11 x 3 inches, 2003. Woodfired.

Dancing Vitamin Jars, Susan's Green and Violite glazes with slip and wax resist decoration, 21 x 5 x 8 inches, 2004.
Woodfired. In the collection of the artist. Appeared in Baltimore Clayworks "Family Matters" Exhibition, 2005.

Blueberry Vase, white stoneware with slips, Violite glaze and wax resist decoration, 4 x 5 x 11 inches, 2004. Woodfired.
In the collection of Mr. and Mrs. Rich O'Neal.

Cattail Vase, Temokku glaze, slips, wax resist, 4 x 5 x 11 inches, 2004. Woodfired. In the collection of Mr. Gary Portnoy.

Rolled Rim Casserole, Tan Gold Ash glaze and slips, 10 x 8 x 8 inches, 2001. Woodfired.

Ocean Jar, white stoneware with Haynes Blue glaze, 5 x 5 x 11 inches, 2000. Soda fired. Appeared in "Explorations in Clay," Nassua Community College Invitational, 2001.

Giving Yourself a Lesson

Blue Soy Bottle, porcelain with
Haynes Blue glaze, 3 x 2 x 6 inches, 2000. Soda fired.
In the collection of Sara Patterson.

My goal as a teacher has always been to help students develop their own techniques, visual sensibilities and methods of working, so that ultimately they will be able to give themselves a lesson. I offer my own working process as an example in order to lead students to think about theirs. I hope this section of the book will do the same.

When I come into my studio, I always find that I have to putter around for a while. I remake clay, check my calendar, look at deadlines and orders and go over my "making list" before I start to work. I like to work from a list, as it keeps me organized, but I also allow myself to stray from it as new ideas come to mind. I find that after I have done some puttering, my head is clear of other concerns and I can settle down to work more easily.

I usually start by thoroughly wedging up as much clay as possible. If you are reading this essay, you probably already know how important it is to wedge thoroughly to remove all the air and inconsistencies from your clay. After wedging I cut the clay open to check how it looks. When hand-building I find that I can avoid some wedging, as the process of making coils or slabs also serves to wedge the clay.

After wedging, I mark each ball of clay with its weight. I go by weight to determine the size and kind of items I make, so labeling by weight lets me know which balls of clay are right for which items.

I find that clay to be used for throwing is best kept on the softer side, which puts much less wear and tear on the wrists and arms. For hand-building and making handles I find that slightly stiffer clay works better. In my studio I keep different bags for harder and softer clay and often label those too so I can remember which is which. To help keep your clay soft, always double-bag it and enclose it tightly in a plastic container. If you have a stiff bag of clay that you want to soften, a good method is to cut the clay in slices as thick as bread, let them soak in warm water for a few minutes and then put them back in your plastic bag. A few hours later the clay will be ready for rewedging. Spending time keeping your clay the proper consistency will pay off!

If you are not sure what you want to make, spend some time going to museums to look at old pots, or find books with pictures of historical pots and make rough sketches in a notebook. Go and look at as many vessels as you can; that is where a wealth of ideas are. I believe that whether you are hand-building or throwing, the work should always start with an idea and go from there. The idea decides the building method.

If I had to choose the most important piece of advice I could give, it would be to work in a series. Whether you are a beginner or an intermediate or advanced maker, working in a series is the way to improve your skills and keep improving your pots. If you are a beginner, your series might consist of three or four vessels. If you have more experience, try and make a series of ten or more. The aim is not to make every pot exactly identical, but to work over and over on the same basic form in order to understand what slight variations can do. There are many advantages to working in this manner. Repeating the movements of your hands and body promotes memorization of the physical aspects of making and the pressure needed in your pulls. By making many versions of a similar form you can introduce subtle changes in shape that will improve your knowledge of form and function. One good exercise is to make five three-pound vases, varying the lip or foot of each one slightly.

When your series of pots is finished, trimmed and leather hard, take the next step in giving yourself a lesson, which is to give yourself a critique of your own pots. Line your series up on a shelf or counter where you can see them well without clutter. Relax, sit down and really look at your pots. Start by asking yourself which pots you like best and which the least. Then decide why this is. Which lip and foot do you like, and why? Which form has the best volume and which surface do you like best? Why do you like what you see? Thinking about these questions as you look at your series can really help you succeed. If you have a trusted friend or colleague you may want to include him or her in the process. But it doesn't stop here. Once you discover what you like from your series, plan another series using what you liked from the last one. In this way you are refining and improving your skills and visual abilities, and the work progresses.

During your throwing or hand-building you will discover certain techniques that you find challenging: pulling or finishing a lip, for instance, or making an even coil. You must spend some time concentrating on the exact point that you find difficult. Do it over and over. Perhaps you can decide not to save any pots until you have mastered that technique.

I do hope that you will try this method of working, and that you will be positive and sup- portive with yourself. I find that learning to work with clay is a journey that is never ending. When I reach one plateau, I know there is another that I want to travel to, and that it will take time to get there. Remember that this is not an instant process, and enjoy it.

Glazing

I have found that students generally do not enjoy glazing. It is difficult to learn because the results are not immediate: no freshly glazed pot looks anything like it will after the firing. Experience and patience are key, but the following techniques might help ease your start:

1. Stir your glaze thoroughly and often, as it will settle.

2. Make sure you have enough glaze. You will need almost an 8,000 gram bucket full in order to glaze easily.

3. Before glazing, wax the bottoms of all your pots carefully with hot or cold wax. Try using the inexpensive foam straight-edge brushes available

Oval Jolly Jar, white stoneware with Red Yellow Green slip glaze and stamped decoration, 5 x 4 x 10 inches, 1999. Woodfired.

at most hardware stores; it's relatively easy to make a good straight line with them. Wash the brush with warm water soon after using it and you can reuse it for a while. If you are glazing for a wood, salt or soda firing, it is better not to wax the bottom of your pots, because the wax will make it difficult to glue on the wadding.

4. After waxing, look at all your pots and decide which glaze or glazes to use on each before you begin to work. You can write directions to yourself in pencil right on the pot. The pencil marks will burn away in the firing. This will allow you to get your decisions out of the way before you begin, so you can give your full attention to your glazing methods.

5. Glazing tongs are most useful for small to medium pots, cups and bowls. In general, the best way to use them is to hold the pot near the lip with the tongs and push down into the glaze until the pot is totally submerged. Count to 5 or 6, pull the pot out and pour any glaze out of the interior. Through trial and error you will learn how to get the exact thickness of glaze for the results you want. For a thin application, just dip the

pot in and out. For a thicker application, hold the pot in the glaze longer.

6. Always clean the bottom of your piece thoroughly of any glaze drips when the glaze has dried. After glazing, handle your piece carefully and do not hold it at the lip because the glaze will chip easily there.

I hope these methods will be of help to you as you follow your own path toward making better pots. I also highly recommend the reading list that follows. These books have been very helpful to me.

Recommended Reading

Bayles, David, and Ted Orland. *Art and Fear: Observations on the Perils (and Rewards) of Artmaking.* Santa Cruz, CA: Image Continuum Press, 2001.

Berensohn, Paulus. *Finding One's Way with Clay: Pinched Pottery and the Color of Clay.* Dallas: Biscuit Books, Inc., 1997.

Beittel, Kenneth R. *Zen and the Art of Pottery.*
New York: Weatherhill, 1989.

Clark, Garth. *A Century of Ceramics in the United States: 1879–1979.* New York: E.P. Dutton, 1979.

Chappell, James. *The Potter's Complete Book of Clay and Glazes.* New York: Watson-Guptill, 1991.

De Reyna, Rudy. *How To Draw What You See.* New York: Watson-Guptill, 1996.

French, Neal. *The Potter's Directory of Shape and Form.* Iola, WI: Krause Publications, 1998.

Hluch, Kevin A. *The Art of Contemporary American Pottery.* Iola, WI: Krause Publications, 2001.

Hopper, Robin. *Functional Pottery: Form and Aesthetic in Pots of Purpose.* Iola, WI: Krause Publications, 2000.

Ilian, Clary. *A Potter's Workbook* (Iowa City: University of Iowa Press, 1999). Don't miss this book. It contains the best description I know of throwing techniques.

Leach, Bernard. *A Potter's Book.* London: Faber & Faber Ltd., 1945. This is the bible, still relevant today.

Lewis, David. *Warren MacKenzie: An American Potter.* Tokyo: Kodansha International, 1992.

Peterson, Susan. *The Craft and Art of Clay.* Upper Saddle River, NJ: Prentice Hall, 2003.

Sources

The Potters Shop, 31 Thorpe Road, Needham Heights, MA 02194, 617.449.7687. Great source for pottery books. Their catalog is simple, but good. This is also the source for my favorite potter's knife.

Bennett's Pottery Supply, 431 Enterprise Street, Ocoee, FL 34761, 800.432.0074. Great source for equipment at the best prices.

left: Weighing the clay before wedging.

right: I begin work by wedging clay, forming it into balls, weighing each one and writing the weight on the pieces. This way I know what piece to use for for each pot that I am planning.

I try to keep my studio orderly and clean. I find it easier to work productively in a clean environment, and a clean studio is healthier than a messy one. Clay dust is a serious health concern for people who work with clay. Always wet mop your work space and never sweep, as that puts small particles of dust in the air that are bad for your lungs.

left: It is a good idea to cut your clay open and check for air holes. If there are holes, slap the clay down on the table cut side out and continue to wedge.

right: I try to keep my tools and clay within easy reach of the wheel. But it is important to remember to get up from your work periodically to stretch your body.

Oval Dish with Double Lip

The following instructions are to be carried out with your wheel moving at a fast to medium speed.

upper left: Center a two- to four-pound piece of clay and open it, leaving a thick bottom.

lower left: Open more, keeping the foot of the pot more narrow than the lip.

upper right: Your goal is to throw a V-shaped bowl.

lower right: As you throw, keep your lip rather thick.

upper left: Always take the water out of the inside of your piece as you go so that the clay will dry evenly.

lower left: I like to use a small blue soft rubber rib to make a swirl in the bottom inside of the piece.

upper right: With a wooden tool, clean the bottom of your piece, but don't undercut it.

lower right: To create your double rim, hold a wooden tool steady in your hand with the whell moving slowly. Supporting the rim of your piece, push straight down into the rim with the point of the tool, dividing your rim in two. Your fingers should be moist when you do this.

upper left: Carefully throw each side of your double lip. Do not pull too thin.

lower left: Pull your wire under your pot, being careful to hold your wire down to the wheel head as you pull it across.

upper right: With the wheel stopped and with clean palms, firmly press in on the sides of your V-shaped bowl until it forms an oval shape that you like.

lower right: Using your fingers, gently pinch and move the clay wall to create additional design elements. There are many ways to do this, so just experiment!

upper left: Come back to your pot when it is leather hard. Center the bottom on the wheel head as you would any pot.

lower left: Place coils carefully around the longer sides of the pot and put a small ball of clay under each end so that the point doesn't rock.

upper right: Trim a small amount of clay off the outside bottom.

lower right: Trim as much as possible out of your bottom. This is why it is important to remember to leave the bottom thick as you are throwing the pot.

upper left: Your pot should still be soft enough to gently press in on the sides and reestablish your oval.

lower left: With your pin tool, mark where you will cut to create side feet about three inches wide on the bottom of your piece.

upper right: Draw a half moon on the side of your piece defining where you will cut.

lower right: With a sharp knife, cut down until the point of the knife reaches the inside bottom of the foot.

upper left: With the knife angled as shown, make your half-moon cut.

lower left: Measure the opposite side to be the same as the first side, and make the same cut. Note that working on a turntable and a piece of foam is very helpful.

upper right: Make a small handle for each end of your oval. Experiment with different types until you find what you like.

lower right: Flashing slip is applied to those areas that will not be glazed. Flashing slip is liquid clay slip that is used in wood, salt or soda firings to enhance the effect of the kiln's atmosphere. You may choose to decorate over flashing slip with any high-fire slip or the "Fish Sauce" slip recipes listed in the glaze recipe pages at the end of this chapter.

I enjoy decorating this dish in different ways.

Double-Lipped Oval Dish, white stoneware with Susan's Green glaze and slips, 8 x 4 x 5 inches, 2004. Woodfired.

Box with Fern, white stoneware with Amber Celadon glaze and wax resist decoration, 5 x 5 x 7 inches, 2004. Woodfired. In the collection of Mrs. Copper Newman.

Making a Squared Box from Thrown Forms

One of my favorite pieces to make is a softly squared box made from thrown forms. I first learned to make boxes from Michael Simon, who makes exquisite ones that are quite different from mine. It took a number of years of making to develop my own style of box. I hope you try this project, as you will learn many new ways of handling clay that you can use in other pieces. As always when altering clay, it is important to use soft clay when throwing and not to throw your pieces too thin.

left: Center your clay (perhaps three to four pounds) to the width you would like the piece to be and allow your clay to slope straight down to the wheel head.

right: Open your clay to the width you would like your piece to be, leaving a one-inch thick bottom. You will later make cut feet from this bottom.

upper left: Make sure that you compress your bottom well after opening.

lower left: Throw your walls as you would make a cylinder, keeping the walls straight, the bottom thick and enough clay in the lip to make the flange (or gallery).

upper right: If you compress your rim thick and flat you will be able to make your flange more easily.

lower right: While supporting the walls of your cylinder, use your thumb to press down on half of the width of your rim, creating your flange. If it is too thin it will crack when you make your square.

upper left: Create a true flat corner for your flange. This will allow your lid to sit well.

lower left: I like using a soft blue rib to create the surface that I prefer. It is important to me to capture the feeling of the wet, moving clay in my surface.

upper right: Always get the water out of the bottom of your piece with a sponge on a stick. This allows for even drying. You can easily make this tool yourself.

lower right: With your wheel stopped, using only your left hand, draw your middle finger up the inside wall of your piece to create a corner in the clay. Practice will lead you to discover the proper pressure. When you reach the flange, stop moving and use your thumb to gently push out the corner. Now use this technique directly across from the first corner in order to create the second corner.

upper left: With the wheel still stopped, place the other corners between the first two.

lower left: Gently pull on the corners to correct your square and make it more pronounced.

upper right: As your piece dries slightly, gently square the sides and top, as clay has a memory and will tend to return to its original round shape.

lower right: Measure with calipers as shown to determine the size of your lid.

upper left: Using about one and a half pounds of clay for your lid, flatten your centered piece to be quite wide relative to the width of your calipers.

lower left: Open your lid, leaving the bottom less than a half inch thick.

upper right: Throw a small flat bowl, not letting the walls or rim become too thin.

lower right: I like to finish the inside of the bowl with my favorite blue rib.

upper left: Make sure that your lid is as wide as your caliper measurement.

lower left: Note the shape of the lid.

upper right: When your bottom piece is a soft leather hard (but not mushy), it is time to trim. Center the bottom as you normally would for trimming.

lower right: Trim out an interior circle of clay, leaving about a ⅜" rim on the outside. The outside wall of your pot should stay straight. Do not allow it to curve in.

upper left: After you have completed your trimming, the walls should be soft enough to allow you to gently press in to flatten them and square your piece again.

lower left: Trim your lid when it is still soft enough to bend without cracking.

upper right: Trim your lid flat on the bottom and gently sloping on the sides.

lower right: I like to smooth the clay after trimming to compress the grog in the clay.

upper left: Now you are ready to cut the feet on your square bottom. First mark the four corners of the pot; they will be at the center of each foot. You will need a sharp knife to make these cuts. Carbon steel works better than stainless steel. The potter's knife sold by the The Potters Shop is a perfect knife for this (see "Sources" in this section).

lower left: Cut down, stopping at the inside bottom of your piece. Note where the X is marked; these are the areas you will be cutting out.

upper right: After cutting down on each side, remove your knife and cut straight across the bottom to create a squared corner.

lower left: Finish cutting on all sides, making an effort to cut down to the same point each time in order to create an even foot. This takes some practice. Don't expect to get it perfect the first time you try it. I suggest that you throw a few squared pots just to practice cutting.

upper left: Lay a small strip of heavy plastic over the top of your square, then place your lid upside down on top of it, positioning the lid evenly in the middle of the opening.

lower left: Press down gently on the corners of your lid. It should make a soft mark that will help you later.

upper right: Slide your knife in right at the top of the rim and trim your lid on all sides without cutting into your rim.

lower right: The cut clay is now scrap; lift it off your piece and set it aside. Mark the side of your lid and the outside of your bottom so you will know how the lid best fits. Then use your plastic strip to lift the lid out of the vessel. You will probably have to trim your lid again later, so keep the plastic strip under it so that you are able to lift the lid in and out. This kind of lid usually only fits in one way.

upper left: Trim your lid as needed and note the marks that may appear on the top side. They can be a guide for you. If the lid is too wet you may need to let it air dry for a couple of hours.

lower left: Gently shape the lid with your hands in order to help it fit better.

upper right: Gently press your lid into place in your flange, keeping the plastic strip in place. Once I get to this point I usually let the pot sit in place overnight and then check the fit the next day, cutting more as necessary.

lower right: Add whatever kind of handle you like. Note the key that marks how the lid fits.

I like to bevel the bottom cut edges very slightly for a fine finish.

This pot is a lot of work, but I enjoy making it. I hope that it can teach you some valuable techniques.

Box with Weeds, white stoneware with dark slip and Tan Gold Ash glaze, 5 x 5 x 7 inches, 2002. Woodfired.

Trimming Bowls Properly

A common problem I see my students having with bowls is an incorrect placement of the foot. Ideally, the inside and outside of your bowl will match. It is also important to create a relationship between the lip and the foot of your bowl. For instance, if my rim is quite angular, my foot will be also. Or if the rim is soft and rounded, my foot will be too. The following is a guide to help you find the correct placement of your foot and really enhance the form of your bowl.

above: Measure the inside of your bowl with your calipers, placing them at the spot where your curve advances. Of course this point is open to interpretation, but just use your best judgment. This is where the outside of your foot ring will be placed. Naturally, the wider your bowl is, the wider this point will be. Just follow the inside of your bowl.

upper left: After your bowl is centered on the wheel head for trimming, use the measurement you have taken from the inside of your bowl to mark the spot where the outside of your foot ring will be placed. Then mark the spot where you will put the inside of your foot ring, keeping in mind the width of your upper lip.

lower left: Trim your bowl as you normally would. If your pots are on the softer side of leather hard, the trimming results will be better.

upper right: Leave enough clay at the bottom of your bowl to make a generous foot. A taller foot makes for a nicer form aesthetically as well as giving you more to hold onto when you are glazing.

lower right: The inside of the foot ring should be as deep as the outside of the foot ring.

left: The foot ring is finished.

right: The graceful curve of the bowl is enhanced by the proper width of the foot ring.

Bowl with Green Butterfly, dark stoneware with Shino and green glaze, 14 x 14 x 5 inches, 2002. Woodfired. In the collection of Mr. Doug Chilcott.

Glaze and Slip Recipes

Cruet Set, white stoneware with slips,
Amber Celadon and Carribean Sea glazes, 2000. Woodfired.

Woodfire Cone 10 Glazes

Buttermilk
G-200 Feldspar	.29 g
Flint	.24 g
EPK	.7 g
Gerstley Borate	.10.5 g
Dolomite	.7 g
Whiting	.9 g
Talc	.13.5 g
Bentonite	.2%
TOTAL	.100 g

Rob's Green
Gerstley Borate	.5.2 g
Whiting	.18.3 g
Cornwall Stone	.73.5 g
Copper Carbonate	.10.3 g
Bentonite	.2%

Oestriech Shino
F4 Feldspar	.42.3 g
Spodumene	.35 g
EPK	.5.9 g
Soda Ash	.9.4 g
Neph Syenite	.3.5 g
Ball Clay	.3.5 g
Bentonite	.2%

Oestriech Temmoku
Custer Feldspar	.48 g
Whiting	.11.6 g
EPK	.5.4 g
Flint	.20.1 g
Zinc Oxide	.2.3 g
Spanish Red Iron Oxide	.8%
Bentonite	.2%

Nick's Misfire
Neph Syenite	.40 g
Whiting	.15 g
Talc	.10 g
Grolleg	.15 g
Flint	.10 g
Tin Oxide	.10 g
Copper Carbonate	.1%

Old Yellow

Neph Syenite . . . . .639 g
Dolomite . . . . .211 g
Zircopax . . . . .160 g
OM4 Ball Clay . . . . .43 g
Red Iron Oxide . . . . .10 g
Bentonite . . . . .30 g

Red Yellow Green Slip Glaze

Redart . . . . .70 g
Whiting . . . . .30 g
Bentonite 2%

Mackenzie's Amber Celadon

Apply this glaze very thin.

Alberta Slip . . . . .33 g
Wollastonite . . . . .13 g
Custer Felspar . . . . .20 g
Gerstle y Borate . . . . .3 g
Whiting . . . . .7 g
EPK . . . . .3 g
Flint . . . . .14 g
Yellow Ochre . . . . .7 g
Bentonite 2%

Violite

This is a light sky-blue celadon.

F4 Feldspar . . . . .40 g
Flint . . . . .30 g
Whiting . . . . .20 g

Colemanite . . . . .10 g
Dolomite . . . . .5 g
EPK . . . . .10 g
Manganese Dioxide .1 g
Cobalt Carbonate . . . . .25 g
Bentonite 2%

Tan Gold Ash

Alberta Slip . . . . .50 g
Whiting . . . . .30 g
EPK . . . . .15 g
Rutile . . . . .5 g
Bentonite 2%

(Use thin fake ash.)

Woodfire Flashing Slips

Helmar Flashing Slip

A good place to order Helmar is from Archie Bray (406 442 2521).
Mix this slip to the consistency of milk. Apply to leather-hard clay by dipping or brushing. Color is orange to tan to cream.

Helmar . . . . .2000 g
EPK . . . . .800 g
Neph. Syenite . . . . .800 g
Flint . . . . .400 g
Bentonite 2%
TOTAL . . . . .4000 g

Bauer Flashing Slip

Mix to consistency of thick milk. Apply to leather-hard clay or to bisqueware by brushing or dipping. Color is mahogony orange to golden brown.

Soda Ash . . . . .5.7 g
Zircopax . . . . .10.5 g
EPK . . . . .41.9 g
Kentucky Ball . . . . .41.9 g
Bentonite 2%
TOTAL . . . . .100 g

Pete's Dark Flashing Slip

This is a darker brown slip. Apply as above.

Ball Clay . . . . .500 g
Red Art . . . . .500 g
Bentonite . . . . .2% g
TOTAL . . . . .1000 g

Have fun!

Woodfire Decorating Slips

Fish Sauce

You must know this one! Use on leather-hard clay or bisque!
You can use all the colors over all flashing slips, but be aware that green does not work very well.

I use 8 grams of cobalt carbonate to I cup of fish sauce for a nice medium blue.

This slip can be used from cone 04 to cone 11, on greenware or bisqueware.

Grolleg . . . . .582 g
Flint . . . . .208 g
F4 Feldspar . . . . .313.2 g
Pyrophyllite . . . . .104 g
Bentonite . . . . .125.2 g
TOTAL . . . . .1332.4 g

Michael Simon's Blue/Black

Use for decorating on leather-hard clay. I love it—it becomes like glaze!

Albany Slip or Substitute . . . . .95 g
Neph. Syen. . . . . .5 g
Cobalt Oxide . . . . .5 g
Bentonite 2%
TOTAL . . . . .105 g

Tudball's Rutile Slip

Use on leather-hard clay. Colors are mustard, tan and dark yellow.

Custer Feldspar . . . . .10.5 g
Talc . . . . .10.5 g
Ball Clay . . . . .21.0 g
EPK . . . . .32.6 g

Flint . . . . .26.3 g
Rutile . . . . .15.0 g
Bentonite 2%
TOTAL . . . . .115.9 g

White Pearl Slip
Sagger XX Ball Clay .30 g
Tile #6 Kaolin . . . . .10 g
F4 Feldspar . . . . .15 g
Flint . . . . .15 g
Bentonite . . . . .2 g
TOTAL . . . . .72 g

The Best Black Decorating Slip
Duncan E-Z Stroke #012 or 013 . . . .1/2 teaspoon
Water . . . . .3 drops

Wax Resist
      Important: This resist is for lids only.
Do not use for wax resist decorating.

Wax . . . . .1 cup
Alumina Hydrate . . . . .1 heaping tablespoon

Stir well.

Green Soy Bottle, white stoneware with Susan's
Green glaze, flashing slip and wax resist, 3 x 5 x 7
inches, 2004. Woodfired.

Dragonfly Bowl Set, Susan's Green glaze and slips, 2004. Woodfired. In the collection of Mrs. Copper Newman.

Dragonfly Pitcher, Susan's Green glaze and slips, 5 x 7 x 9 inches, 2004. Woodfired.

Rolled Rim Casserole, Tan Gold Ash glaze, 8 x 10 x 9 inches, 2000. Woodfired.

Ash Glazed Jar, Tan Gold Ash glaze, 5 x 8 x 10, 1999. Woodfired. Juried into the Ceramics National Exhibition in 2001. In the collection of Mr. and Mrs. Howard Howland.

Jar with Ash Runs, dark stoneware with Tan Gold Ash glaze, 5 x 5 x 8 inches, 1999. Woodfired. In the collection of the artist.

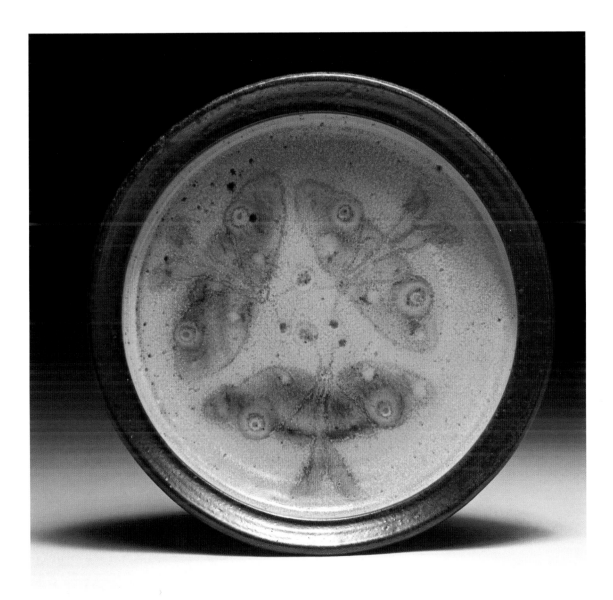

Lunar Moth Platter, dark stoneware with Old Yellow glaze and green glaze, 13 x 13 x 2 inches, 2000. Woodfired. Juried into the Strictly Functional Pottery National Exhibition. In the collection of the artist.

Milky Way Platter, dark stoneware with Buttermilk and Haynes Blue glazes, 12 x 12 x 3 inches, 2001. Woodfired.

Jar with Leaves, white stoneware with Susan's Green glaze and wax resist, 5 x 7 x 11 inches, 2003. Woodfired.

Contemporary Woodfiring in the USA: A Brief History

Rabbit Teapot, white stoneware with Tan Gold Ash glaze and dark slip, 5 x 7 x 8 inches, 2000. Woodfired. In the collection of the artist.

Tradition and Chance

Around the mid-twentieth century, a number of artworld trends began to point to a new awareness of the aesthetic potentials of an expanded field of experience. Action painters threw materials at their canvases, other painters gave up painting altogether in favor of Happenings made out of groups of people, conceptual artists dematerialized their work to talk about making meanings instead of objects: People seemed to be attempting by very different means, and with different ends in view, to find ways for visual art to exit its traditional boundaries in order to enter and address a wider reality. Two aspects of this shift in thinking contributed to what was to become a resurgence of the traditional craft of woodfiring pottery in the United States.

The first was a reconsideration of traditional crafts as practices that could be taken up by fine artists. As many self-imposed barriers began to be questioned, distinctions separating fine from applied and high from low became more fluid. In the late 19th and early 20th centuries, the European influence of the Arts and Crafts and Bauhaus movements set the stage for a reevaluation and elevation of craft and its artistic potential in the United States. As the Bauhaus dissolved under Nazi persecution, many of its key figures fled to the United States, bringing with them an influx of Bauhaus rigor, talent and philosophy.

Marguerite Wildenhain, a master potter who had trained at the Bauhaus and then assumed directorship of its ceramics department in Dessau, moved first to the Netherlands and then to the United States after Nazi purges barred her from German academia because of her Jewish heritage. In California she established the Pond Farm school, where she led influential intensive summer workshops from 1949 until 1980. Wildenhain wrote extensively, lectured and conducted pottery workshops throughout the United States at the height of her career, spreading a dogma based on total commitment and an integration of art and life.

In 1933, Black Mountain College was founded in North Carolina with a mission to create an experimental and interdisciplinary learning environment with a combined emphasis on fine and liberal arts. A number of Bauhaus educators—among them Josef and Anni Albers and Walter Gropius—came to teach at Black Mountain after emigrating to the United States.

Recognized as a major center of American cultural innovation by the 1940s, Black Mountain was also informed by Bauhaus ideals, which envisioned a unified field of fine and applied arts. Karen Karnes, who led Black Mountain's ceramics department along with her then-husband David Weinraub in the 1950s, combined a thorough knowledge of traditional techniques with modernist thinking.

This was a cultural moment at which it became possible to understand forward-thinking experimentation and the revival of craft traditions as closely linked. By the 1970s, it had informed a generation of artists and educators. Small craft centers throughout the United States—Penland School of Crafts, Pilchuck Glass School, Peters Valley Craft Education Center and others—were either expanding their traditional roles or being newly founded and developing a base of support.

In the meantime, increasing numbers of craft traditions were on the wane or threatened by extinction all over the world. Woodfiring was one of these. Just as it was dying out as a viable form of industrial production in the few remaining places in the world—most of them in Asia—where it was still practiced as such, woodfiring began to acquire new life as a form of specialty in the West. Artists such as Peter Voulkos began woodfiring and brought to prominence an aesthetic specific to the techniques employed. As information and knowledge about woodfiring began to spread, increasing numbers of people with very different backgrounds and practices began to engage with it. The result was a network of devotion and obsession that grew stronger as more woodfiring kilns appeared throughout the country and the distinctive look of their products became more familiar.

The second relevant aspect of mid-century paradigm shifts was the new interest in the aleatoric—in exploring the ways that processes and effects determined by chance could influence or shape a work of art. John Cage's work in the world of music promoted chance as a strategy in ways that rippled beyond composing with sound. (Cage was also an instructor at Black Mountain.) The idea of allowing something to happen and being attentive to the result, rather than viewing the creative process as primarily an exercise of the will, gained increasing

acceptance. As many Western artists were noticing by this point, this idea was new to the arts only in the West, while it was deeply embedded in many Eastern aesthetic sensibilities and practices.

One of the aspects that makes firing pottery with a wood-fueled kiln unique is the extraordinary opportunity it affords for the exploitation of chance. The natural course of the wood fire and the variables it introduces can produce sublime and not entirely predictable visual results. An aesthetic that prizes these aspects of the firing is often labeled Japanese, since it is the Japanese woodfiring tradition that was historically the most enamored of these potentials and their effects. While numerous woodfiring traditions have informed contemporary American practice, the Japanese tradition—especially that part of it that is interested in facilitating rather than repressing the aleatoric effects of the fire—had a crucial role in shaping the renewed interest in woodfiring in America. This is no doubt partly due to political and world historical circumstances, as the Chinese tradition is also ancient and influential, and woodfiring continues to be practiced on a large scale in China today. But while China remained relatively off-limits to ordinary Americans until recently, World War II brought American soldiers into close contact with Japanese culture, and the GI bill funded their study in the arts when they came home.

In 1970 ceramist and scholar Daniel Rhodes described his perceptions of the philosophical basis for the Japanese aesthetic in *Tamba Pottery: the Timeless Art of a Japanese Village,* a seminal work that reflected the changing attitudes that led to the growth of contemporary American woodfiring. Describing a centuries-old style of pouring glaze that he witnessed practiced in Japan, Rhodes wrote:

"We are confronted here with 'action art' more than three hundred years old. There seems to be no parallel in Western ceramic art. In all the long history of ceramics in the West, the potter has been more in the position of one who carefully directs and controls the processes of his craft, rather than one who collaborates with the raw materials in the directions in which they seem to naturally tend. There is a fundamental difference between the two approaches. In one the potter stands above his materials and works his will on them; in the other he accepts the materials and the process as his partner" [1]. Rhodes connects this understanding of materials and processes to cultural attitudes regarding the role of nature in the act of making:

"Kiln firing in Japan has always been regarded as something of a natural process, and the action of the kiln accepted much as the geologic processes of the earth are accepted for their results. What we might regard as accident is thought of more as natural happening, to be appreciated on its own terms rather than in relation to any set standard. The pot may have its *kami,* embodied as the sum of all the events that have shaped it. And the pot may be considered not so much a static object as a record of the play of various forces" [2].

Chance and Nature

Natural conditions beyond the control of the potter contribute significantly to the results of woodfiring. Because the sheer labor and the investment of time and resources woodfiring requires is so great, potters who commit to it must decide that there is something unique to woodfiring that they cannot reach by any other means. And to be engaged in any kind of woodfiring is undeniably to interact with forces of nature larger than oneself. In a sense it is the phenomenon of the fire that retains the ultimate authority over the process and its results. A crucial part of the outcome will always be up to the fire to determine, regardless of the level of human expertise and experience involved. In some traditional contexts an attitude of reverence and respect toward natural processes is a given. In the context of contemporary Western ceramics, this attitude assumes the quality of a specific aesthetic: All the parts of the process that are within human control serve to support the occurrence of the awesome moment at which nature inevitably takes its course and transforms the willed endeavour of the individual.

A number of technical factors contribute to this condition. A wood fire's effect on glazing provides just one example of the complexity involved.

The fire is started at the mouth or entrance to a loaded kiln and built up gradually over a period lasting from several hours to several days, eventually reaching very high temperatures at which flames fill the chambers of the kiln and touch every pot (unless it is protected from direct contact with the fire by being placed inside another vessel, which is called a sagger). During the course of the fire, ash settles and gathers on the pots. The type and quantity of ash that reaches a pot will vary depending on where the pot is placed in relationship to the primary source of the fire. When fires reach temperatures high enough to completely burn the wood that fuels them, converting all its hydrocarbon content to gas, the part of the ash that remains is composed only of the less than two percent of the wood consisting of elements such as alumina, potassium, sodium and silica. As the kiln reaches very high temperatures, these elements melt and form a vitreous coating that bonds to the fired clay. A wood fire, given the right conditions, produces a naturally occurring form of glaze: A highly volatile, active, impermanent state of matter, carefully guided to reach its extreme, changes into one of the most stable, permanent, durable states of matter.

Depending on the kind of wood used, the duration and intensity of the fire, the placement of the pots and the way the fire touches them as it spreads through the kiln, the appearance and thickness of this natural glaze can vary dramatically. At its least prominent it forms a very thin, barely perceptible coating that seals the surface of the fired clay. Its color can range from neutral to intense in value. Long firings that consume a great deal of wood will result in a greater accumulation of ash on upper surfaces of the pots, which will create thicker glaze that can lead to drips and streaks that run down the pot as the glaze melts and flows. Ash also interacts with glazes applied before the firing, producing new colors and effects. Every pot that has been touched by the fire emerges from a woodfired kiln with a unique surface hue and texture that exists as a record of its interaction.

Nature and Current Conditions

At the time of writing woodfiring continues to grow in popularity. The first woodfiring conference in the United States, sponsored by the Japan Society, was held in 1982 and attracted about 40 participants. Since then three more conferences have been held in the United States; the most recent one, which took place in 1999, was organized as an international forum and brought 450 participants from all over the world, including 50 panelists and presenters from 15 countries.

One of the reasons why the resurgence of woodfiring has been particularly strong in North America is because wood is still readily available here, while it has become a scarce resource in many areas of Asia that were formerly woodfiring centers. Industrial kilns worldwide have turned to less expensive and more efficient, if also less exciting, fuel sources. But the market for the distinctive quality of woodfired ceramic wares continues to exist, and so the practice and its traditions continue to be maintained on a smaller and more studio-oriented scale throughout the world.

Given the cultural climate in the United States, where a short historical memory and an ever stronger sense of hybrid eclecticism tend to dilute the strength of tradition, it is safe to say that woodfiring has spread primarily through social contact, passing from person to person much in the way that fire leaps from one piece of wood to another. This is an easy way for it to catch on, because woodfiring is practically if not absolutely dependent on the social: it is almost impossible to engage in alone, relying as it does on extensive resources, group labor and the kind of arcanely detailed technical, intuitive and practical knowledge that can best be exchanged by working together with others over long periods of time. In general, people who woodfire start by contracting the curiosity and the addiction from others, and tend to want to pass it on.

In this sense the rise of woodfiring reflects a trend that takes us back to much older models of artmaking and of productive human efforts in general. The group effort is as desired as it is necessary. In this context people labor physically side by side, stay up for long hours and make difficult decisions together for the sake of a creative outcome in which they are all invested. The social situation parallels the natural one: in both, the individual relinquishes some degree of control in order to reap the benefits that can stem from collaboration.

Grace Sullivan

Provincetown, Massachusetts, 2004

Vase with Ferns, white stoneware with Susan's Green glaze and slip, 5 x 5 x 11 inches, 2004. Woodfired. In the collection of Peter Kelman and Therese Magreau.

References

1. Daniel Rhodes, *Tamba Pottery: The Timeless Art of a Japanese Village* (Palo Alto, CA and Tokyo: Kodansha International, 1970) p. 62.

2. Rhodes [1] p. 63.

Bibliography

"BMC: A Radical Vision," Black Mountain College Museum and Arts Center. http://blackmountaincollege.org/content/view/15/58/

"Bauhaus 1919-33," Bauhaus-Archiv Museum of Design. http://www.bauhaus.de/english/bauhaus1919/index.htm

Clark, Garth. "Karen Karnes, Retrospectively." *Ceramics Monthly,* June/July/August 2004.

Cort, Louise Allison. "The Death and Life of Woodfiring in Asia." *Different Stokes: The 1999 International Woodfire Conference.* Iowa City: Iowa University, 1999.

Hindes, Chuck. "Introduction." *Different Stokes: The 1999 International Woodfire Conference.* Iowa City: Iowa University, 1999.

Moore, Tony. "Passionate Fire." *CeramicsTECHNICAL* 16 (2003).

"Ripples: Marguerite Wildenhain and Her Pond Farm Students," Robert V. Fullerton Art Museum, California State University San Bernardino. http://rvf-artmuseum.csusb.edu/PONDFARM/index.html

Troy, Jack. *Wood-Fired Stoneware and Porcelain.* Radnor, PA: Chilton Book Company, 1995.

Wildenhain, Marguerite. *Invisible Core: A Potter's Life and Thoughts.* Palo Alto: Pacific Books, Publishers, 1973.

"Women's 'Werk': The Dignity of Craft," American Museum of Ceramic Art. http://www.ceramicmuseum.org/exhibitions-events.htm

Rolled Rim Bowl, dark stoneware with Haynes Blue glaze, 8 x 8 x 5 inches, 2000. Woodfired.
In the collection of Mrs. Josee Reboul.

Blueberry Oval Platter, white stoneware with blue glaze and slips, 16 x 8 x 4 inches, 2003. Woodfired.

Fish Vases on Tray, white stoneware with celadon glaze and slips, 9 x 8 x 10 inches, 2003. Woodfired. In the collection of Sara Lyter and Larry Greenspan.

Oval Footed Basin, white stoneware with Green Ash glaze, 12 x 8 x 6 inches, 2004. Woodfired.

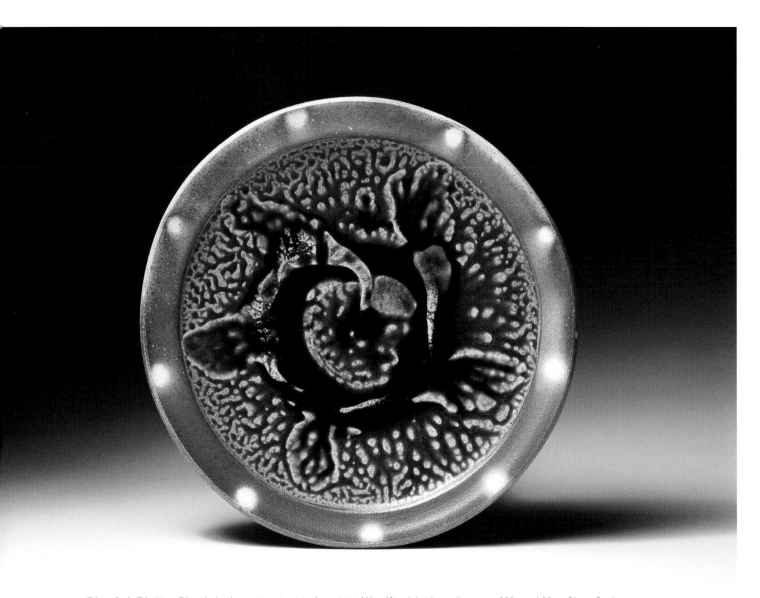

Blue Ash Platter, Blue Ash glaze, 12 x 12 x 3 inches, 2004. Woodfired. In the collection of Mr. and Mrs. Chris Stokes.

Swimming Up Stream Casserole, white stoneware with Red Yellow Green slip glaze and slips, 12 x 10 x 10 inches, 2004. Woodfired.

Where are the Tuna? Teapot with Teabowls, white stoneware with slips and Red Yellow Green slip glaze, 8 x 5 x 7 inches, 2004. Woodfired. In the collection of Ms. Edmee Froment.

Rolled Rim Bowl, green speckled glaze, 12 x 12 x 5 inches, 2002. Soda fired.

Catskill Mountain Platter, Red Yellow Green slip glaze, Blue Ash glaze and Buttermilk glaze, 12 x 12 x 3 inches, 2004. Woodfired.
In the collection of Mr. and Mrs. Michel Goldberg.

About the Contributors

many of this country's leading contemporary artists and was delighted to collaborate with Susan Beecher on this book.

Ranley Bent is a Facilities Manager in a New York city advertising agency who also has a passion for fire. He is thankful for the chance to put his pyromania to good use.

Carolyn Chadwick has worked as a hand bookbinder since 1977. Her work—binding books, making protective boxes and portfolios and making decorative boxes—is fairly solitary, so she completely enjoys joining the woodfiring crew to help stack and stoke the kiln goddess.

Julie Crosby is a professional potter who graduated from the Hartford Art School in 1995 with a BFA in Ceramics. She has been an Artist in Residence at the Worcester Center for the Arts, The Mendocino Arts Center and Louisianna Tech University. She has built nine kilns and is currently at work on another.

As the proprietor of The Soho Photographer since 1974, **D. James Dee** specializes in photographing works of art in New York City. Over the years he has worked closely with

Bruce Dehnert earned his MFA in Ceramics at Alfred University. He has taught at Hunter College and Parsons School of Art and Design in New York City, the School of Art in New Zealand, and the Universiti Malaysia Sarawak on the Island of Borneo. Bruce has exhibited widely and his work is included in numerous collections, including those of the White House and the Yixing Museum of Ceramic Art in China. He is currently Head of Ceramics at Peters Valley Craft Center in New Jersey.

Maureen Donovan received a BFA in Ceramics from Tyler School of Art in Philadelphia. She has taught art at an alternative high school and is currently a teaching assistant in Ceramics at Sugar Maples Center for the Arts in Hunter, New York. She loves to woodfire and does so as often as she can with Willi Singleton and Susan Beecher.

Nick Gaeta graduated from the University of Hartford with a degree in ceramics. He has built approximately 13 wood and gas firing kilns. He lives with his wife and two girls in Cape Cod, where he builds houses.

Tania Kravath is a ceramic artist whose work is shown in New York City at Ceres Gallery. She maintains studios in Manhattan and in West Hurley, New York. Her work encompasses themes of family relationships, immigration and community. She currently teaches at Sugar Maples Center for the Arts.

Carol Grocky Lewis earned her MA from New York University and subsequently studied with many notable artists, including Frank and Polly Ann Martin. She currently teaches ceramics at Marymont Manhattan College and at the 92nd Street Y in New York city. Her work has been accepted into numerous national juried exhibitions. She shares a group ceramics studio in New York City with Tania Kravath and Susan Beecher.

Steven Morowitz graduated from the University of Hartford in 1995 with a degree in Ceramics. He spent a year at Penland School of Crafts focusing on functional woodfired pottery. Eventually he set up his own pottery and wood kiln in upstate New York and today is the owner and operator of "The Urban Potter."

Sara Patterson is a co-founder of Queensboro Potters in New York City. She teaches pottery in New Jersey and New York and her work has appeared in numerous national exhibitions. She finds that firing the wood kiln lends a good balance to her otherwise urban existence.

Barbara Ravage, a health and medical writer, is the author of nine books. What she really loves, however, is throwing pots. She has had the good fortune to know Susan Beecher as a teacher for a brief time and as a friend for many years. A native New Yorker, she now lives on Cape Cod.

Grace Sullivan is an installation artist who has been designing books for Catskill Press since 2003. She received an MFA in Sculpture from Cranbrook Academy of Art and has exhibited her work in Finland, Michigan, Rhode Island and Massachusetts.